• HALSGROVE DISCOVER SERIES ➤

SECRETS *of the* HIDDEN SOURCE

In Search of Devon's Ancient and Holy Wells

TERRY FAULL

HALSGROVE

First published in Great Britain in 2004

British Library Cataloguing-in-Publication Data
A CIP record for this title is available from the British Library

ISBN 1 84114 354 5

HALSGROVE
Halsgrove House
Lower Moor Way
Tiverton, Devon EX16 6SS
Tel: 01884 243242
Fax: 01884 243325
email: sales@halsgrove.com
website: www.halsgrove.com

Printed and bound by D'Auria Industrie Grafiche Spa, Italy

Contents

Author's Note and Acknowledgements   5

Introduction   7

A Time Line of Key Events   10

Chapter 1   Sacred and Healing Waters: The Origins of Devon's Holy Wells   11

     Table 1   Holy Wells healing traditions   14

     Table 2   Anglo-Saxon well place names   20

     Table 3   Domesday well place names   23

     Table 4   Traditional uses of Holy Wells in Devon   28

Chapter 2   The Holy and Ancient Wells of Devon   29

     Map showing: Holy Well locations in Devonshire   30

     Table 5   Most significant wells in each district   31

     Torridge District   32

     West Devon District   51

     Greater Plymouth and South Hams District   74

     Teignbridge and Torbay District   84

     Exeter and East Devon District   99

     Mid Devon District   108

     North Devon District   114

Chapter 3   The Early Celtic Church in Devon   133

     Table 6   Dates when Celtic Church dedications

        were first recorded   138

     Map showing: Churches dedicated to Celtic Saints   139

Bibliography   144

To my family past, present and future

Author's Note and Acknowledgements

As a child I played amongst some ruins just a few hundred yards from my home and recent excavations have now shown these to be the remains of the well chapel of Fenton-Ia, established by St Ia of St Ives, one of the 6th century Celtic Saints. Every Sunday I visited my grandparents' cottage for which a source of drinking water was one of the wells linked to this site. I was fortunate enough to have a career which took me to every parish across Cornwall and Devon and this deepened my love of the history of the countryside and of the maps that interpret what can be seen on the ground. One of my work colleagues in the late 1970s was the late Jack Meyrick who was visiting Holy Wells in Cornwall, after he published his book on this work, we discussed his approach to the subject on a number of occasions.

I have lived in several parts of Devon and was struck by the occasional references to a Holy Well to be found on maps or in local histories but it appeared that no detailed study was available for Devon to rival the many publications on similar places in Cornwall. In 2002, an award from the Tarka Country Millennium Awards enabled me to make a study of Holy Wells in Tarka Country around Dartmoor and Exmoor and from this I developed the idea of a county-wide book.

Any historical research worker will find that much of the ground of intended research has already been covered by others. I too found that many had gone before and I acknowledge a significant debt to those such as Theo Brown, sometime folklore recorder for the Devonshire Association, to numerous authors of parish and church histories, and to the unknown surveyors of the Ordnance Survey. Others such as Lawrence Hunt, Debbie Lang-Trengove and Carol Marshall have worked on Devon's Holy Wells and I have learned much from them and from the authors of the many books published about the Holy Wells of Cornwall and elsewhere. The research facilities at the Tavistock Subscription Library and the West Country Local Studies Library at Exeter have been invaluable. I am grateful to Kate Jordan and Richard Pedrick of the

University of Bath for advice and encouragement and to The Churches Conservation Trust and The Orthodox Church News for permission to use some of their illustrations. Sarah and Martin of Eye to Eye Design and Tom of TD&M have provided valuable help with my faltering attempts at digital photography. I am grateful for all the support from everyone who has contributed to my knowledge and given encouragement and especially to the Tarka Country Millennium Awards for sponsoring the project which led to this wider study. Special thanks to Joanna FitzGerald for her support, encouragement and advice throughout.

To the landowners who gave permission to cross their land, my thanks. That a place which has been visited by pilgrims for centuries but is no longer open to all, is an issue for discussion elsewhere and is a matter which local communities might like to consider. This book identifies those sites with public access but anyone who plans to visit any of the others should seek permission before they venture on to private land.

This book draws heavily from many sources and the bibliography lists the main references I have used. The fieldwork, photographs and interpretations are mine alone and I take full responsibility for any inaccuracies or misleading statements. This is not an academic treatise on Holy Wells; for that you will have to look elsewhere. However, I hope readers will find something new about Devon's history and want to discover more.

Perhaps something included here, a picture a description or even a memory will encourage your own pilgrimage of discovery.

Whether you use the information in this book to plan a good day out at a beautiful spot, to go in search of healing or spiritual refreshment, I believe you will find it; perhaps you will also gain something from the mystery of place which can still be felt at many of Devon's Holy Wells.

Introduction

This is a book to use and enjoy in several ways. Firstly it describes which of Devon's many thousands of water sources have been credited with powers of healing, fortune telling, and as places to make contact with spiritual forces. Secondly it is a guide to where these Holy Wells are still to be found and suggests that a visit to them will take you to some of the least-known and unspoiled parts of the county.

For thousands of years and throughout the world, certain natural springs and wells have long been places of pilgrimage and worship. Devon has a rich heritage of over two hundred such sites where in times past, people would come in search of help, guidance and reassurance. Today we are beginning to re-discover and value affinity with the natural world and Holy Wells are some of the places where this can be found.

They are often in remote and beautiful areas but sometimes a well is now in a wholly urban setting where passers by are often unaware of the history at their feet. Indeed one ancient well at Tavistock is a feature under glass in a busy hotel lounge! I hope the photographs and descriptions in this book will encourage you to visit some of these special places for yourself. You will be following in the footsteps of pilgrims who, for hundreds and perhaps thousands of years, have journeyed along these same pathways.

As we shall see, Devon's Holy Wells acquired their status for a number of very different reasons and over many centuries. The jumble of information which makes up our history is often difficult to unravel and the timeline on page 10 may help give a context of the key events which influenced the use of Holy Wells in this part of the British Isles. Amongst scholars, there is no agreed definition for a Holy Well and so for the purposes of this book, the following description has been used to decide which of the many thousand of wells should be considered:
'a well or spring having a tradition of healing or spiritual significance or where there is evidence for ancient origins'.

Also included are some wells of ill-omen (Cadio's Well at Bradford (Well 11) and Lidwell at Dawlish (Well 56), and a few examples of more recent wells of interest.

The gazetteer in Chapter 2 lists the wells in local authority and then in parish order; this provides a logical method of grouping and should help when planning to visit some of the places identified. For the most interesting sites, a National Grid reference using the Ordnance Survey Explorer series of maps is given, together with a note about the well and my understanding about public access to the site. The traditions associated with a well are given but I make no claim (or expect no credit!) for the healing, fortune-telling or spiritual powers of a particular water source.

St Nectan's Church, Stoke.

This book also introduces a fascinating but neglected aspect of the county's history. Most people know about the 5th and 6th century Celtic Saints of Cornwall but Devon too shared in this Age of Saints. The influence of these early Christians in the history of county has often been overlooked and, according to some authorities such as the eminent late 19th century clergyman and antiquarian the Rev. Sabine Baring-Gould, may even have been actively suppressed. Many modern historians believe that Baring-Gould and certain later writers, had an overly romantic view of the Celtic Saints but St Nectan, St Petroc, St Brannoc and others are still with us in well names and church dedications across the county. Some of these Devon Saints and their Holy Wells became locally, nationally and even internationally important; the shrine of St Nectan at Stoke was decorated with gold and silver and precious gems, and was endowed with gifts from the Saxon King Athelston of Wessex.

At Chittlehampton, the money from generations of pilgrims visiting St Urith's Grave and Holy Well made the church there one of the wealthiest in the area.

The invading Romans, then the Anglo-Saxons, and later the medieval English church, all played a role in the development of certain springs of water as Holy Wells and their use as places of worship, for healing and the pardoning of sins. Their influences are still to be found in the well names of Devon. Place name evidence is a fruitful field of study for the local historian and is one of the sources I have used in my research. Written and oral traditions are also valuable sources of information but while local residents can be of use, sometimes they may be mistaken or even misleading. In one parish I was told that a particular well could no longer be found but some fieldwork eventually located it close to a public footpath behind the village church. At another tiny church, a member believed that the nearby Holy Well was no longer used but I was later assured that water from it had been in the font at a baptism some six months previously when some sixty people were present in the congregation.

Many of the wells described in this book are springs of fresh water with little evidence remaining of man-made structures around them. Others such as at Welcombe and Romansleigh have simple well houses made of local stone and a few, such as Leechwell at Totnes, St Gudula's at Ashburton, St Brannoc's at Braunton and Holy Well at Broadclyst, are substantial shrines which rival the Holy Wells of Cornwall, Brittany and Ireland.

Whatever the evidence remaining above ground, the Holy Wells of Devon are amongst the oldest places which have a direct link back to the early history of the county. A few have official recognition and protection as listed buildings but for many, the traditions associated with them are becoming forgotten, the well neglected, and some have even been destroyed. It would be a shame if, in our time, we allowed our Holy Wells and the traditions around them, to fall into further neglect and disrepair. One note of caution however; contrary to popular belief, few of Devon's Holy Wells have absolute proof of an unbroken line of continuity from pagan to early Christian and onward to modern times. Traditions and history have become jumbled with folklore and any attempt to disentangle the stories can only uncover part of the true picture. Nevertheless our Holy Wells are real links with the past and in many towns and villages, the site of the Holy Well is far older than the church or any other remaining building. I hope this book may encourage more local people and organisations to follow the example of some Devon communities who have already restored and continue to use their Holy Well.

The sites are spread across the county but with the greatest concentrations in the west and north. This may be because these were the last areas of the kingdom of Dumnonia (Cornwall, Devon and West Somerset) to be conquered by the Saxons before they banished the influence of the native Celts, with their saints and affinity for Holy Wells, back beyond the River Tamar. Perhaps here in the more remote areas, the old customs lingered longest and hence into the historical records. Possibly the distribution simply reflects the perennial problem for the researcher, that the areas you know best and visit often, produce the most information. Whatever the reasons, there is no doubt that the tradition of the Holy Well is to be found throughout Devon and I expect that the sites listed in this book will be added to by time, further research and local intelligence.

St Urith's statue on Chittlehampton church.

A Time Line of Key Events

Age of Celtic Saints in Devon and Cornwall when many wells and churches were first used for Christian worship

APPROX. DATES	EVENT	MATTERS OF PARTICULAR NOTE
600BC	Celtic peoples in Dumnonia (Cornwall, Devon and West Somerset)	
AD43	Romans arrive in Britain. Exeter established c.AD55; Legion outposts at North Tawton, Tiverton, Okehampton, Axminster	AD313 Rome recognises Christianity as an official religion
410	Roman control of Britain ends	
446	British citizens appeal unsuccessfully to Rome for help against invading Saxons/Angles	Dumnonia under Celtic rule and not yet subject to Saxon invasion
460–600	Celtic Christianity already established in Dumnonia St Brannoc teaching in Braunton St Nectan at Hartland St Petroc founds monastery at Padstow Inscribed memorial stones erected Augustine arrives in Canterbury sent by Pope to convert the Anglo-Saxon kings	King Arthur is killed at the battle of Camlan but St Petroc survives and travels in Devon Augustine demands Celtic Christians in West Britain fall into line with Rome
614	Saxons defeat British Celts at Axminster and move west	
664	Synod of Whitby	Celtic Christianity overruled in favour of Rome
675	Much of East Devon becomes part of Saxon Wessex	Minster at Exeter c.690
710–739	Saxon Bishop of Sherborne instructs Celtic Bishop in West to conform to Roman church practice	Saxon Minster established at Crediton
780	Saxons reach Tamar	
816	Council of Chelsea	Teaching of Celtic Christianity outlawed
851	Devonshire first recorded in Anglo-Saxon Chronicle as Defnascir	
927–931	Athelston drives Celtic community from Exeter	West bank of Tamar fixed as Cornish boundary
934	Athelston gives land to St Nectan's monastery at Hartland	Prayer to St Nectan credited with saving Athelston's army from the plague
974	Tavistock Abbey founded close to Cornish border	Abbey dedicated to St Rumon – his bones are brought from Cornwall
963	Clergy encouraged to extinguish worship at wells	Royal command from Canute 'it is a heathen practice to worship at wells'
1043	Celtic Bishopric of St Germans is united with Saxon Crediton	Combined Bishopric moved to Exeter
1066–86	Norman Invasion – Domesday Book	Contains 37 well place names

Sacred and Healing Waters:
The Origins of Devon's Holy Wells

Water is essential for all living things. Every human settlement needs a source of drinking water and in these days of instant water from the tap, and bottles from the supermarket, it is easy to forget just how important it was to have access to a good natural water supply. In Devon, a shortage of water has seldom been a problem: one inch of rain falling on one acre of ground equals 100 tons of fresh water and so, with an average rainfall of 45 inches over the county's 2588 square miles, every year more than 7 billion tons of water falls on to the land. Much of this runs off in the rivers and streams which flow north and south to the sea; some of the rainwater is taken up by vegetation and the rest is absorbed by the soil and rock formations. Some will travel along underground aquifers to be released to the surface when impervious layers meet more porous rocks, or where hydrostatic pressure pushes it up through cracks and fissures. This groundwater is the source for the springs and wells which are marked everywhere on the large scale Ordnance Survey maps of the county. Some springs appear and disappear depending on underground water levels; in the Westcountry springs are said to have 'broken' when they reappear after a dry time. The majority of Holy Well sites are not places in the 'Ding-dong bell, Pussy's in the well' sense of a deep shaft down to the water but are spring-fed, shallow natural or man-made basins.

In Devon, the traditions which have made a place a 'Holy Well' are clearly linked to reasons other than it being a simple source of water. One feature which most have in common is that they are said 'never known to have run dry' and this suggests that the springs which feed them, draw from deep sources (a few wells are now dry but this seems to be due to recent building or other man-made disturbances underground which have diverted the flow of water).

Although it is essential for survival, water can be a negative force; it can take life. It has a mysterious side: sometimes gentle and cleansing, sometimes raging in torrents with the power to sweep all before it. Springs bubble from the ground as if by magic – if you try to stop a natural spring the water will always find a way around any obstruction you put in its path. Alongside its cleaning and refreshing qualities, water holds the power to transform itself; as ice it becomes solid, as snow it is lighter than air. It has the ability to shape-shift into the form of any space which can hold it.

Little wonder then that in many cultures across the world, water was believed to have spiritual power. In India water from the sacred River Ganges is kept in Hindu homes as a living symbol of faith. Water is important in Chinese mythology and the ancient Greeks valued Delphi where two springs were associated with the powers of the Oracle to foretell the future. In pagan northern Europe, particular rivers, wells and springs were believed to be presided over by water-spirits who could grant protection and favours to those who honoured them. Worship at sacred water sites was central to the beliefs of the Celts who occupied much of Britain several centuries before the birth of Christ. When the Romans arrived, they adopted some of the native sacred places as centres for their water cults.

Places such as springs and wells which were already important in local culture, and to which the people gave some allegiance, were convenient points where new Roman gods and ways of worship could be introduced. The coming of Christianity to Devon in the 5th and 6th centuries and the later role of the church as a temporal as well as a spiritual power, influenced the way in which local communities used their Holy Well.

At times forbidden and at others actively promoted, the freedom to value these special places has gone through many changes. Particular water sources may have become a Holy Well for many reasons and this may have occurred at various periods in times past. Very little evidence about the early use of Holy Wells in Devon has made its way into written history and so we are left to interpret clues from local traditions, place names and what little documentation there is.

This chapter looks at some of the influences in the history of the county which have shaped the way in which the Holy Wells in Devon may have been used. It suggests that these should be placed alongside the local traditions and stories that have been passed down through the generations. Some historians tend to discount stories for which there is no definite proof. They are sometimes rather scornful of traditions which suggest that a particular Holy Well is linked to an early Christian saint who took over a centre of pagan water-spirit worship. The truth is that we cannot prove many aspects of history from the time before contemporaneous records were made (the lives of the saints and other early texts on which so many histories rely, were themselves written several hundred years after the events and deaths of the people they describe).

Influence of the Celts

Celtic spirituality was grounded in nature and the cycles of the seasons; life, death and re-birth were all around and confirmed the inter-connectedness of all things. The Celts believed that after death, there was the possibility of entry to the 'Otherworld' – the place of eternal life and reincarnation:

'It is a most delightful land of all that are under the sun; the trees are stooping down with fruit and with leaves and with blossom. Honey and wine are plentiful there; no wasting will come upon you… you will never see death or lessening…'
(Described in Celtic myth by Niamh of the Golden Hair).

As part of the continuity between the everyday and the world of the spirits, the Celts believed that there were places where the 'Otherworld' was close; such places included the points where certain springs of pure water sprang from the earth with their own life force. In modern science-fiction terms, these springs were 'portals' between one world and another and they became centres for veneration and worship.

Every aspect of the landscape was important in Celtic culture. Their sense of the spirit of place was strong and they believed that at sacred locations it was possible to influence the powers which determined whether individuals and their society lived in peace and plenty, or were to be overcome by enemies and a failure of the harvest. In addition to water sources, sacred places and objects might include groves of trees, special hills, plants such as the oak tree, vervain and mistletoe, and animals such as the hare. All were credited with special powers which could influence man's destiny.

To the Celts healing was essentially a spiritual art, and so places associated with the world of the spirits also held the potential for healing. They believed that the cycle of the seasons and the rhythm of nature could influence their own health and wellbeing. There was a right time for all things; certain activities were appropriate depending on the time of year, on the times of sunrise and sunset and on the waxing and waning of the moon. These were all factors which affected when a particular place might have the power of healing. Visiting at the correct time and in observation of the proper rituals were important aspects of the cure. The eve of the summer and the winter solstice (21 June and 21 December), the spring and vernal equinox (20 March and 22 September), together with the festival of Beltane on 1 May, were particular days when the powers of the sacred springs could be used most effectively. Using prescribed words, circling the well in the ordained way or the casting of offerings into the water as supplication or appeasement, might be involved. No detailed excavation of a Holy Well has been made in Devon but elsewhere, offerings of coins, inscribed stones, jewellery and bones have all been found at Celtic water ritual sites. Healing is a physical and an emotional process. Some natural water sources do contain minerals which may influence health; substances such as calcium, sodium, magnesium and potassium occur naturally and some water is rich in iron (chalybeate springs) or sulphur. In certain districts of Devon, very low levels of the radio-active gas radon can be detected at the mouth of natural springs.

Although the traditions associated with some Holy Wells have been lost, we do have information about the claims made for about half of them. About 60 per cent of these were credited with powers of healing. The range of conditions is given in the following table:

Holy Wells healing traditions.

Condition for which well was visited	Percentage of all wells used for healing
Cure for problems of the eye	54%
Skin complaints	5%
Cure for scurvy	4%
Cure for fevers	4%
All ills	33%

These beliefs were part of the heritage of the Celtic people who ruled Devon before the time of the Romans and up until the coming of the Saxons some six centuries later. We have very little factual information about these people, known as the Dumnonii, but we know they were a tribal society with strong traditions intertwined with the world of the spirit and their gods. The area called Dumnonia covered the regions which have since become Cornwall, Devon and part of West Somerset, but the tribal societies found here lived lightly on the land and evidence of their long occupation is not always easy to find. Less than 1 per cent of place names in Devon can now be traced back with certainty to the language of the Celts. Their word for well or spring was fenton or venton and a sacred grove was known as nemeton; later Celtic words include lann and eglos to describe a holy place. These words occur in place names such as Landkey (lan of St Key), Feniton (boundary water) near Honiton, Venton (fenthon) near Dartington, several other venton locations such as those near Chagford, Crapstone and Ivybridge and in the nemeton places such as Nymet Tracey and Kings Nympton.

Influence of the Romans

In AD43 the Roman army under Claudius entered Britain and within a dozen years had reached as far west as the River Exe in the land of the Dumnonii. They established a regimental headquarters for part of the Second Augustan Legion at Isca (Exeter), with forts at places such as North Tawton, Okehampton, Tiverton, Cullompton and Axminster. Smaller military stations were at Ide, Countisbury, Alverdiscott and a number of other strategic points of communication. The Dumnonii are said to have been friendly to strangers and certainly they do not seem to have posed any long-term military threat to the Romans. Within twenty-five years or so the legion had left Exeter for Gloucester. Work began at Isca (to be known as Isca Dumnoniorum) on the construction of the buildings for the civil administration of Dumnonia and although there is still much to learn about this period of Roman rule, it probably saw the exercise of power through support of local tribal chiefs and strong trading arrangements based on the administrative centre.

The Romans seem to have been content for the tribal structure and customs of the Dumnonii to continue, and it is notable that in Devon and Cornwall there is very limited evidence for centres of sustained direct occupation. At Isca Dumnoniorum, the Romans made use of the natural springs to provide water for the public bath house, and archaeological evidence suggests that at least one well, close to the present cathedral site, was used as a shrine.

Across Britain, the invaders took a pragmatic view of the native population's adherence to nature deities and indeed they often adapted what they found to suit their own religious practices. For example, at Aqua Sulis (Bath) they took over the sacred springs and re-dedicated them to their own goddess, Minerva.

Although there was no such significant sacred site in the area of Dumnonia, it is worthy of note that one of the Roman forts outside Exeter at North Tawton, was called Nemetostatio, meaning the 'outpost at the sacred groves' Examination of maps shows that within a few miles of the North Tawton Roman site, and along the rivers Yeo and Mole (old names, the Nimet and Nemet), there are five nymet or nympton i.e. sacred grove place names and a significant number of settlements incorporating the words beer or beara, the Old English words with an equivalent meaning to the Celtic nymet. The site at Nemetostatio could house over a thousand soldiers so it was clearly felt there was a need for a substantial military presence in the area of the sacred groves.

There is also a suggestion that a Holy Well at Torrington was named after Coventina, which may indicate a link with the Celtic goddess of wells of that name at Carrawburgh near Hadrian's Wall, where a Roman temple complex was dedicated to her.

A pantheon of deities came with the first Romans. Though Christianity eventually spread throughout the Empire, at first it existed as another form of religion alongside the veneration of older gods. While the Celts tended to think of their gods and nature spirits as beings who needed to be placated and even feared, the Romans saw the influence of the gods at a more mundane level. They could be approached for help in matters of everyday living, and even asked for favours in return for worship, and so there was a need for places where such supplications could be made.

By AD313, Christianity was recognised across the Roman Empire as an 'official religion' and there can be little doubt that it influenced many of the leading Roman citizens in Britain. Eventually a Christian community developed in Exeter and, although the importance of the town was somewhat in decline by the middle of the 5th century, the Christian message would have reached most parts of Devon during this period. We cannot know what influence it had but, like most things Roman, it probably had the greatest impact amongst those tribal chiefs and traders who wanted to find favour with the 'powers that be' at Exeter. The coming of the Romans and the first introduction of Christian teaching probably did very little to change the belief of the Dumnonii that springs where pure water constantly flowed from the earth, were indeed gateways to the eternal.

Although the Roman occupation of Britain is said to have ended in AD410, in fact the influence of Rome had been declining for several decades before this.

The legions had withdrawn and an appeal went to Emperor Honorius for military aid; this was refused and in effect the citizens of Britain were told to look to their own defence. In the century since the acceptance of Christianity by Emperor Constantine, the Christian Church had prospered so that most of Southern Britain was at least nominally Christian. The end of direct influence from Rome saw a flowering of a British Church which was much influenced by the Celtic culture in which it developed. In Celtic society there was little idea of individual ownership of land; tribal chiefs and even the kings of larger groupings, were in effect elected and charged to pursue the common wealth of the whole community. These ideas translated easily into the pattern of Celtic Christianity which owed much to the teachings of Martin of Tours (AD316–397), one of the first bishops of the church, who advocated simplicity, humility of heart, dignity and courtesy, that all possessions should be held in common and that members of the church community should value quiet prayer and seek honour from no man. Another important influence on the British Celtic Church was the monastic tradition of the Orthodox Church (the Eastern Roman Empire arm of the Christian Church based in Constantinople and which became the Greek and Russian Orthodox communities). An interesting echo of the link with the Orthodox Church is that four of Devon's Saints who have Holy Wells associated with them, St Nectan, St Brannoc, St Urith and St Sidwell, are still remembered in the Orthodox Calendar of Saints, and each has a holy icon representing them.

Icon of St Nectan.

The leaders of the Celtic Christian Church looked to the teachings in the Gospel According to St John as their source of inspiration. This presents the story of Jesus as a symbol of the everlasting struggle between light and darkness and suggests that this is a challenge that everyone must face. John's Gospel contains a number of important references associated with the power of sacred water in baptism and healing:

At the sacred pool at Bethesda: *'…lay a great multitude of impotent folk, of blind, halt, withered, waiting for the moving of the water.'*
(John Chap.5 v3)
The curing of blindness at the pool of Siloam: *'…Go, wash in the pool of Siloam. He went his way therefore, and washed, and came seeing.'*
(John Chap.9 v7).

The relevance of these stories would not have been lost on a people whose traditions also taught of the power at sacred springs. The Saints of the early Celtic Church who first told these stories to the people were very important in the development of Holy Well sites in Dumnonia.

Plaque at St Gudula's Well, Ashburton.

Carved head from Lanhadron, Cornwall.

The traditions which credit the water from so many Holy Wells as being an effective cure for problems associated with the eye may be a metaphor for the impact of these Gospel stories. Conversion to Christianity through baptism with holy water was presented as a new way of seeing *'...that they which see not might see...'* (John Chap.9 v39) – away from the darkness and towards the Light of the World. It is easy to understand how, over many centuries of oral tradition, many Holy Wells became associated with improvements in sight.

Two Holy Wells in the county commemorate early Celtic Christian martyrs who are unique to Devon. Traditions from the 6th century tell how St Urith of Chittlehampton and St Sidwell of Exeter were beheaded with harvest scythes by local people and of how springs of pure water rose from the places where they fell. Although these are local saints, the association of a severed head in their stories is very much in the wider Celtic tradition. The head was believed to contain the essential essence of a person's being and symbolised spiritual power; carvings of heads occur in many Celtic cultures.

Influence of the Anglo-Saxons

The unsuccessful plea for aid to Emperor Honorius in the early 5th century, arose from the increasing incursions into Britain by raiding Angles, Saxons and Jutes. In fact these groups made slow progress; this was the period in history when the first legends of King Arthur describe him as a strong military leader who united the Christian British tribes and kingdoms to resist the heathen invaders. It was more than 250 years before the Saxons captured Exeter. In these long centuries a Christian Church flourished in western Britain. Its origins may have begun with the teachings which were introduced by the Roman Christians, and was helped by links with Christians in another Celtic country, Galatia (in the area which has since become Turkey), who were part of the Orthodox tradition. However its strength and development were largely as a result of the message spread by the holy men and women who travelled out from the great teaching monasteries of Ireland and Wales, and who landed on the western coasts of Devon, Cornwall and Somerset. Natural springs close to the places where these travellers settled were used for practical and religious purposes and their association with them is remembered in dedications to those such as St Nectan, St Petroc and St Brannoc. The influence of the Celtic Saints in Devon is considered further in Chapter 3.

At the time of their first settlement in Britain, the Angles, Saxons and Jutes were pagan. In AD597 Pope Gregory sent a mission under Augustine to convert the new Anglo-Saxon kingdoms which had become established here; he did so knowing that there was already a native British Church. However the Pope and Augustine seemed to have taken the view that this Celtic Church was doing too little to convert the Saxons to Christianity. Augustine did make contact with the Celtic Church leaders (two meetings were held and the first of these was somewhere near the mouth of the River Severn), but they found his insistence that they abandon many of their practices and submit to his and Rome's authority, arrogant and unacceptable. Whilst the leaders of the native church may have been ready to accept Augustine converting the Anglo-Saxon kings, they probably took the reasonable view that his role did not include taking over control of the existing church structure which was now embedded in the culture of the native peoples. The British Church already had abbots, bishops and clergy who held that its practices were in keeping with Christian teachings and their understanding of the faith which had been agreed by the founding fathers of the Church at the Council of Arles in AD314 and the Council of Nicaea in AD325. They believed that Rome was moving away from the fundamental articles of the faith which had previously been shared by all traditions of the Christian Church.

Augustine and other missionaries sent from Rome continued to work in the Anglo-Saxon kingdoms. By AD675 when the Saxons took final control of much of the eastern territory of the Dumnonia, they had largely accepted Augustine's message and the Roman tradition. And so, although the native Celtic people in Devon were not subject to the pagan influences which some other parts of Britain experienced with the first coming of the Anglo-Saxons, they were now subjected to pressure to conform to Canterbury and Rome. In addition, these conquerors came to settle and to claim ownership of the land and the reception they received from the Domnonii was probably less friendly than that which had greeted the Romans some six centuries before. In AD682 following a decisive Saxon victory, when the British Celts were 'driven in flight as far as the sea', the whole of North and West Devon fell into their hands.

Despite this piece of early propaganda, it is probable that much of the native Devon population stayed put to live alongside their new masters. Some indeed remained in positions of local influence and we can perhaps see an example of this in a charter of AD739 in which King Athelheard seems to have excluded Celtic lands at Treable (Tryfedal) near Cheriton Bishop from a grant of land to one of his Saxon thegns. Force of arms and gradual assimilation increased the Saxon hold on Devon and by AD927, King Athelston was able to expel the remaining Celts from Exeter. This was described by William of Malmsbury in dramatic terms *'he attacked them with great energy, compelling them to withdraw from Exeter until which time they had inhabited on a legal equality with the English. He then fixed the left bank of the Tamar as the Shire boundary'*. We cannot be sure what this ethnic cleansing meant but it probably indicates that any remaining Celts to the east of the Tamar, and who held positions of wealth or power, were deprived of authority and influence. Anglo-Saxon or perhaps more correctly, English, Devon was fully established.

The Anglo-Saxons were not only great fighters and settlers but they also brought efficient administration. From this period of British history written records really begin. Land charters appear which describe in great detail the holdings of large and small landowners (33 such charters for estates in Devon still exist today). As a result of this efficiency, it is Anglo-Saxon place names which are used in the documents and the old Celtic names are either adapted or simply do not appear in the written records. Celtic names such as Trellick, Kernstone, Penstone and Creedy survived and are still to be found on modern maps, but these make up only a tiny proportion of place names in the county.

In looking for evidence of Holy Wells we therefore need to consider the words which would have been used by the Anglo-Saxon Church and landowners to describe special water sources and holy places. The complexity and variations of spelling to be found in the different forms of Anglo-Saxon and Old English means that a number of possible words can be identified. The following table suggests some which may be relevant to the search for Devon's Holy Wells:

Anglo-Saxon well place names.

Anglo-Saxon/Old English word	Probable meaning
Wella/welle/wille/waella	Well or spring
Halig/hael	Holy or omen
Funta	Spring
Bearu/beare/beer	Sacred grove
Run/rum	Secret

The words wella, welle, wille and waella can be identified in many place names across the county but in conjunction with derivations from halig or hael they occur only thirteen times in the English Place Names Survey for Devon; Halwell near Totnes and Halwill near Holsworthy are the best examples. Other place names derived from the Anglo-Saxon words bearu and beer are more common; Beer near Seaton is one example, and we have already seen the number of Beer names close to the River Nymet and the nemeton sacred grove site at North Tawton.

A look at a large scale map of Devon may suggest a number of other possible candidates, for example Hallowell in Bere Ferrers parish (although another explanation for this is that it derives from allerwealla – well of the alders), and Holiwell names such as the farm near Clovelly. The evidence for Holy Wells based on the place names on modern maps needs to be treated with caution and tested against other information.

The Anglo-Saxon Church was efficiently organised and in fact for some time was the only body which held influence across the separate kingdoms of Britain. It was organised in a structure first suggested by Pope Gregory to Augustine, of two provinces each having up to twelve bishops. Although this plan was never fully implemented, the Church under Augustine and his successors at Canterbury was effective in convincing the rulers of the Anglo-Saxon kingdoms that it would increase their authority if they accepted Christianity and allied themselves with Rome. The new bishops sought to consolidate their authority and were mindful that it would have been under-mined if people still believed they could gain spiritual help and guidance from unofficial sacred places such as Holy Wells. These were part of the old Celtic Christian tradition which the Anglo-Saxon Church sought to replace. Successive attempts were made to forbid people using Holy Wells and other centres of spiritual power:

AD990–94 – *Aelfric denounces those who offer gifts to stones, trees or worship at springs.*

AD1005–8 – *the Canons of Edgar decree that clerics must entirely extinguish every heathen practice and forbid worship at wells.*

AD1020 – *Canute declares 'it is a heathen practice if anyone worships idols…wells or stones or any forest tree.'*

Throughout this period, the Celtic Church in Britain was under pressure to conform to Rome. A significant decline in its status began in AD664 following the Synod of Whitby when Oswy of Northumberland, the most powerful Anglo-Saxon king, had called representatives from the Celtic Church and the

Roman Church based at Canterbury to debate the two Christian traditions. On the outcome depended which influence would become dominant not only in Northumberland but in the other Anglo-Saxon kingdoms which were converting to the faith. The case for the Celtic tradition was put by Bishop Colman of Lindisfarne, and Abbot Wilfred from Ripon spoke for Rome. Wilfred argued that the Church in Rome received authority from its founder, Peter, who had been given the keys of Heaven by Christ. Colman did not dispute this but explained that his Church looked to the Apostle John to whom Christ had entrusted the care of his family; according to Colman 'all men are the family of Christ'.

Oswy was known to be sympathetic to the Celtic Church but he was fearful of not being allowed through the gates of Heaven and ruled that the argument should be settled in favour of Canterbury and Rome (a real case of the fear of God being put into someone!). Despite the ruling at Whitby, the Celtic Church continued to have significant influence, and allegiance to its teachings was not replaced in some places for very many years. In its heartlands such as Dumnonia, popular adherence to the old Celtic ways had to be recognised and treated sensitively. More than two hundred years after Whitby, the Anglo-Saxon bishop of the See of Crediton (which had been created in AD739 to minister and oversee the people in Devon and Cornwall), was obliged to recognise the power of Celtic Saints such as St Nectan of Stoke when miracles attributed to the saint were honoured by King Athelston. As late as AD974 the founding of a new Anglo-Saxon abbey at Tavistock took account of Celtic sensibilities when it was jointly dedicated to Mary and St Rumon – a Celtic Saint whose bones were brought from Cornwall to be placed in a shrine in the new abbey building.

The Anglo-Saxons created Devon out of Dumnonia but despite their efficient administration, new language and centralised church structures, they did not succeed entirely in separating the people from attachment to the Celtic Saints and their Holy Wells. The effective governing and tax-collecting arrangements established by the Anglo-Saxons were the foundation for the next invaders who now took advantage of a weakened royal household to press their claim to the English throne.

Influence of the Normans and Beyond

After the Battle of Hastings in 1066, the Normans took advantage of the structures established by the Anglo-Saxons and used them, some twenty years after the Conquest, to draw up the Domesday Book which provided the first detailed account of Devon. Commissioners were sent to every part of the county and in each of the 33 Hundreds (an early sub-division of the land and a forerunner of the parish) the priests, the reeve, and six villagers from every main village, gave evidence about who owned the land and its value before and after the Norman Conquest. This information was checked by four Normans and four local men who were sworn to give account and verify it.

Domesday Book provides us with the names of places across Devon where a well was so important that a settlement took its name from it. There are at least 37 of these places which can be identified from Domesday and although the site of the original wells of 1086 may have been lost, most of the places named can still be traced today:

Domesday well place names.

Domesday name	Probable Modern Name	Domesday Name	Probable Modern Name
Asswelle	Ashwell, Diptford	Pisswelle	Pirzwell, Kentisbeare
Carsewella	Kingskerswell	Ryngeswille	Ringwell, Heavitree
Carswelle	Kerswell, Broadhembury	Sirewelle	Shirwell
Carswill	Kerswell, Hatherleigh	Tottewill	Titwell, Aveton Gifford
Cressewalde	Kerswell, Holcombe Rogus	Gosewelle	Goosewell, Plymstock
Carswella	Abbotskerswell	Merewild	Marwell, Ringmore
Halgewella	Halwill	Cadewile	Kidwell, Uplowman
Gerwille	Gorwell, Hemyock	Bradewelle	Bradwell, East Down
Wedicheswella	Pickwell, Georgham	Gabbewelle	Gabwell, Teignharvey
Walcome	Welcombe	Doducheswelle	Dunkeswell
Wella	Coffinswell	Westwogewill	West Ogwell
Wille Egelf	Edginswell, Cockington	Estwogewill	East Ogwell
Blachewelle	Blakewell, Marwood	Wiflewelle	Winswell, Peters Marland
Sperchewelle	Sparkwell	Crochwelle	Crockernwell
Colewill	Colwell, Offwell	Macheswelle	Monkswell, Sampford Spiney
Cokeswell	Coxwell, Exbourne	Medwell	Meadwell, Kelly
Uffewelle	Offwell	Whytewell	Whitewell, Colyton
Lodeswille	Loddiswell	Noteswelle	Nutwell, Woodbury
Hagewile	Halwell		

An interesting aside to these Domesday well names is that five contain a version of a word which translates as 'kerswell'. This derives from the Anglo-Saxon for 'cress-spring' and suggests that the places where this plant grew or was cultivated had some importance; one of these wells was claimed by the king and one by the abbot. Watercress is an herb which is high in vitamins, is a good source of iron and iodine, has medicinal qualities to cure rheumatism, and which counteracts anaemia and was also used for colds. In a *Materia Medica* of AD77 it is listed as an aphrodisiac. Cress has been cultivated as a salad plant since Roman times and it is clear that the early people of Devon enjoyed its sharp, spicy taste.

Only two of the well settlements in the Domesday list, Halwell (hagewile) and Halwill (halgewella) have hallig type names which suggest a Holy Well. At some period after 1086, other places in the list such as Abbotskerswell, Welcombe, Coffinswell, Marwell and possibly Kerswell, Hatherleigh (if this is St John's Well), and Nutwell, Woodbury (if this is Goldenwell), became known as Holy Wells.

The Normans built on the ecclesiastical structure inherited from the Anglo-Saxon Church. However they changed the strictures which had been imposed against worship at Holy Wells and in 1102 the Council of Westminster issued a canon (church rule or instruction) which said:
    'Cults at wells are to be allowed but subject to the authority of the bishop'.

In effect, the use of Holy Wells as special places was to be allowed under licence and so control over their use was given to the church authorities. During the following centuries numerous other springs acquired status as Holy Wells because of links with the church, monasteries or through local traditions.

From this time, the use and importance of many Holy Wells increased and their fame spread. Offerings from pilgrims who were attracted because of stories about the healing or spiritual powers of a particular well, brought wealth to the local church; in Devon a good example of this is the shrine and well of St Urith at Chittlehampton which became one of the wealthiest in the area from the gifts left by those from far and wide who came seeking forgiveness of their sins and help from the holy maid.

Throughout the Middle Ages new Holy Wells were established close to monasteries, hospitals and leper houses; St Elizabeth's Well at Crediton,

Ladywell at Pilton and St Martin's at Exeter are examples of healing wells associated with nearby foundations which worked with the sick and dying. At other places the tradition of a Holy Well grew up because the land on which it stood was owned by a church or monastic house: the wells at Romansleigh (a manor once owned by Tavistock Abbey) and St Helen's at Croyde (which was a daughter-house of St Mary's Abbey at Pilton) are examples. The offering of gifts and prayers at a shrine was often a genuine act of piety, and those who could not travel to visit the sacred places in the Holy Land or to the important shrines in distant parts of England, would make the journey to a more local holy place.

Increased prosperity in the early centuries following the Conquest saw the building of many new churches and the renovation of many of the older Anglo-Saxon places of worship. Churches were required to be both dedicated and consecrated – dedication is a declaration that the building is devoted to God, and consecration makes it a holy place in the eyes of the Church. As part of the ceremony for the inauguration of a new or rebuilt church, the local bishop was required to consecrate the building by the sprinkling of holy water. In addition it was usual to dedicate the new church to a holy patron, usually a saint, angels or the Trinity. The opportunity of including the Holy Well in the process had the advantage of legitimising its use and providing a reason to encourage pilgrims.

The role of the Bishop of Exeter in dedicating a number of churches to a patron of his choice, sometimes meant that an ancient identification with a local Celtic Saint was replaced by a more acceptable patron from the mainstream of Church traditions. Examples of where this may have happened include Lewtrenchard, now Peter, but probably St Petroc before 1261; Coryton which was dedicated to St Andrew in 1261 but perhaps before this to St Curig (the place is called lancurig in a Saxon missal) and Landkey, now Paul, but probably St Key before 1346. Throughout Devon there are a number of churches where the original dedication is not known and these include Lustleigh, which is the site of a 6th century inscribed Christian memorial stone, and Woolfardisworthy West which is the area once heavily influenced by St Nectan's foundation at Stoke.

The Middle Ages saw a number of chantry chapels erected and these were sometimes associated with a well. A chantry chapel was a place endowed by some wealthy person and where a priest was paid to 'chant' masses for the benefactor and his family. Where such a chapel was constructed away from the parish church, the bishop would often agree to the priest also ministering to local people. Good examples of chantry chapels associated with Holy Wells are at Spreacombe which dates from about 1250, the licence granted by Bishop Laccy in 1424 to Thomas Horlock to celebrate divine service at the chapel of St Petroc in Charles (the well here was built over in the 20th century by the then rector when he built a new study for himself), and also the chapel at Alfardisworthy which was licensed for use by the Tyrell family in the 14th century and which stands within a few yards of a well house.

The association of most Holy Wells with an existing parish church or with the site of a chapel is not at all surprising and supports the view that, in Devon, many of these wells originated either because of a link with the first Celtic Saints or that later church authorities encouraged their use in places where it could influence and benefit. Of the wells studied for this book, there are some significant exceptions to this association with a current or historical consecrated building. These include two remote wells on parish boundaries (Stidwell, Ashburton and Goldenwell, Woodbury), three wells dedicated to St Mary or known as Ladywell (Sticklepath, Lynton and Crediton), and remote wells at Druid's Well Chagford, EyeWell Morthoe, Coverney's Well Torrington, Sister's Well Countisbury, and Holywell Broadclyst (this is near a Beer place name site). It may be that some of these are either pre-Christian water spirit traditions which have survived, that they served as useful boundary points for a land charter, or that an original church or chantry chapel connection has been lost.

Throughout the medieval period, and beyond, the use of Holy Wells for healing and as the centre for local rituals and revels became an established part of life in many Devon communities. The Protestant Reformation of the 16th century saw many of the manifestations of 'popish' practice attacked and destroyed, but there is little evidence to suggest that this was the fate of many of Devon's Holy Wells. The customs associated with these places were rooted in the local community and helped give it identity. This meant that the local Holy Well was treated with toleration, and it was only those people who believed that their status, education or wealth, placed them above the superstitions of the common people, who displayed active hostility. The removal of the shrine at the Holy Well of St Urith at Chittlehampton may be an example of Reformation destruction but it did not succeed in ending local loyalties.

The local rituals grew from folklore of earlier times, an example being the leaving of a small rag torn from a petitioner's clothing tied to a tree close to the well. These 'cloutie' wells were once common and even today there are five places in Devon where the custom survives (or has been introduced): Leechwell at Totnes, Coverney's Well at Torrington, St Mary's Well at Hatherleigh, Fitz's Well at Okehampton, and Libbett's Well at Crediton.

Tantalising mentions of Holy Wells are to be found in documents from various periods of history for example:

- A place called durnawille (the hidden spring) near Cockington appears in 1159 in a boundary agreement of Tavistock Abbey lands, and in 1240 there is mention of Halganwylle in Coleridge Hundred, and in 1249 an Adam de Halegwell lived somewhere in Bampton Hundred.
- Another personal name linked to a Holy Well – Roger de Halghewille appears in documents of 1333, and a year before this there is mention of Halgwille juxta Hexworthy, also in Shebbear Hundred.
- 1576 at Shobrooke – 20 shillings paid for making cleane the well…
- 1727 at Weare Giffard – a well of pure water where the Clerk fetches water for baptisms.

Unfortunately it is has not yet been possible to identify all of the wells to which entries in documents such as lay rolls, charters, church accounts and other sources refer, and there remains some intriguing historical detective work still to be done.

Over time, new ideas and thinking began to influence local customs but, in many places across Devon, an active tradition of the Holy Well continued into the 18th and 19th centuries. The celebrations at Holy Wells were not always quiet affairs; the Holywell Revel on Ascension Day in the parish of North Molton became a village outing with fairground rides and pony-races and continued until the early 20th century.

The traditional customs of the countryside began to attract the interest of anti-quarian clergymen and folklorists and, in the 17th century, a start was made in the collection of some information about local folklore. The parsons of Devon saved many traditions and stories before they were lost by the death of that generation of people who were the last direct link with the old ways. Their interest was sometimes greeted with suspicion and an understandable objec-tion to being labelled as 'quaint' but much of what we know about the Holy

Wells of Devon is due to the efforts of these early local historians. The traditional uses of Holy Wells in Devon are recorded in various sources and a summary of this information is given in the following table:

Traditional uses of Holy Wells in Devon.

Tradition Type	Percentage of all traditions
Baptismal use	24%
Curative powers	60%
Fortune telling powers	16%

A range of stories describe how bent pins, other charms or pebbles would be thrown over the left shoulder into the water, and a wish or request for help would be whispered or chanted.

The evidence from traditions, place names, church records and historical documents does confirm that Devon has a rich heritage of Holy Wells. The reasons why a particular spring became such a special place are many and varied and this chapter has suggested some of the influences involved. Many have been valued by generation after generation, and loyalty to the local traditions has withstood hostility and manipulation from those in authority. However the greatest threat has come from the indifference of the last eighty years. Today, a fresh interest in the heritage of our local communities is beginning and may have come in time to save those Holy Wells which remain.

Historical research is unlikely to answer questions about why our forebears valued their Holy Wells so highly, or whether the waters really did provide healing and spiritual support. In our world it would be easy to dismiss such claims as superstition or the product of simple folk from another age. It is possible however that we can learn something from those who lived closer to the natural world and who believed in powers outside of themselves. We often admire the traditions of other cultures but perhaps at Holy Wells we can still experience a little of the spirit which is our heritage.

The Holy and Ancient Wells of Devon

There are historical references to more than 200 Holy Well traditions in the county. Some of these are now only place names for which there is no other information or evidence on the ground; at other places, the well has been destroyed or lost. This chapter provides a description of the traditions and history of the most significant Holy and Ancient Wells of Devon; those included have been selected because they show the diversity and richness of the Holy Well traditions which can still be discovered by anyone who seeks them out.

The sites are grouped by their local authority area and then by parish. By using these places as a destination for a country walk or car trip, you will find some of the most unspoilt parts of Devon. To help make your discovery of them more enjoyable, a flavour of some of the history and other matters of interest in the parish is included for many of the less-well-known places. Notes about each of the sites listed below are given together with a National Grid Reference to help in finding them. A guide on public access includes hints for those with limited mobility.

Holy Well locations in Devonshire

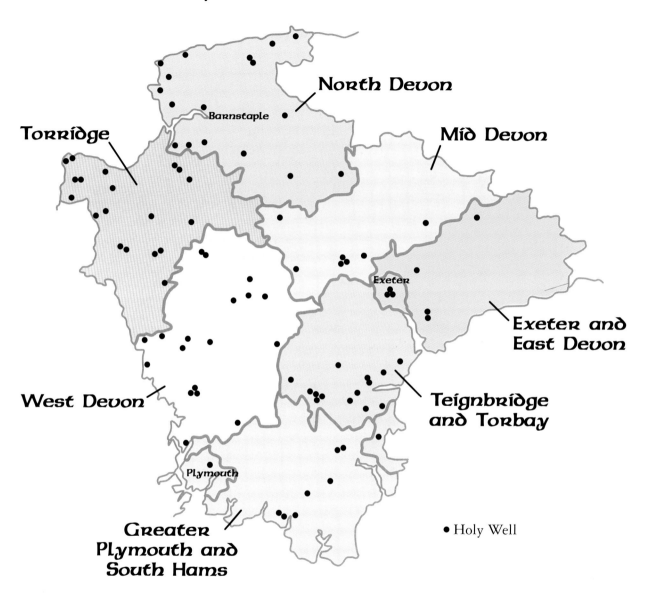

The table opposite lists the most significant wells in each district.

Well number	Parish	Well name
1	Welcombe	St Nectan's Well
2	Hartland	St Nectan's Well
3	Hartland	Bradstone's Well
4	Hartland	St Leonard's Well
5	Hartland	St Clare's Well
6	Clovelly	Holywell
7	Woolsery	Ladywell
8	Bradworthy	St Peter's Well
9	Bradworthy	Alfardisworthy Well
10	Newton St Petroc	St Petroc's Well
11	Bradford	Cadio's Well
12	Bradford	Holemoor
13	Holsworthy	St Mary's Well
14	Holsworthy	St Peter's Well
15	Weare Gifford	Trinity Well
16	Weare Gifford	Cranbury Well
17	Torrington	Coverney Well
18	Petrockstowe	Lane Well
19	Halwill	Chapel Well

Torridge

Well number	Parish	Well name
20	Hatherleigh	St John's Well
21	Hatherleigh	St Mary's Well
22	Coryton	St Curig's Well
23	Lewtrenchard	St Petroc's Well
24	Okehampton	Fitz's Well
25	Belstone	Holy Well
26	Sticklepath	Ladywell
27	Sampford Courtenay	Parish Well
28	Lydford	Fice's Well
29	Tavistock	St John's Well
30	Tavistock	West Street Well
31	Tavistock	Fitz's Well
32	Lifton	Holy Well
33	Bradstone	St Nonna's Well
34	Stowford	Drinking Trough Spring
35	Bere Ferrers	Hallowell
36	Sheepstor	St Leonard's Well
37	Chagford	Druid's Well

West Devon

Well number	Parish	Well name
38	Egg Buckland	St Edmund's Well
39	Ringmore	Marwell
40	Bigbury	St Anne's Well
41	Aveton Gifford	St Milburga's Well
42	Loddiswell	Lodd's Well
43	Halwell	Holy Well
44	Totnes	Leechwell
45	Totnes	Harper's Well

Greater Plymouth and South Hams

Well number	Parish	Well name
46	Ashburton	St Gudula's Well
47	Ashburton	Ladywell
48	Ashburton	Dropping Well
49	Ashburton	Stidwell
50	Widecombe	Saxon Well
51	Bovey Tracey	St Mary's Well
52	Newton Abbot	St Mary's Well
53	Kingsteignton	Honey Well
54	Kingsteignton	Fairwater
55	Bishopsteignton	Whitewell
56	Dawlish	Lidwell
57	West Ogwell	Ogg's Well
58	Abbotskerswell	Ladywell
59	Coffinswell	Holy Well
60	Tormorham	St Elfride's Well

Teignbridge and Torbay

Well number	Parish	Well name
61	St Sidwell	Holy Well
62	St Sidwell	Cathedral Well
63	St Leonards	Parker's Well
64	Broadclyst	Holy Well
65	Dunkeswell	St Petroc's Well
66	Woodbury	Golden Well
67	Woodbury	Village Well

Exeter and East Devon

Well number	Parish	Well name
68	Crediton	St Wynefred's Well
69	Crediton	Libbett's Well
70	Crediton	Ladywell
71	Cullompton	St George's Well
72	Shobrooke	Holy Well
73	Bow	Puddock's Well
74	Cheldon	Church House Well

Mid Devon

Well number	Parish	Well name
75	Rackenford	Holy Trinity Well
76	North Molton	Holywell
77	Romansleigh	St Rumon's Well
78	Chittlehampton	St Urith's Well
79	Tawstock	St Peter's Well
80	Horwood	St Michael's Well
81	Westleigh	St Petroc's Well
82	Pilton	Ladywell
83	Braunton	St Brannoc's Well
84	Georgham	St Helen's Well
85	Morthoe	Eyewell
86	Morthoe	St John's Well
87	Lee (Ilfracombe)	St Wardrede's Well
88	Parracombe	Lady Well
89	Parracombe	St Thomas's Well
90	Lynton	Ladywell
91	Countisbury	Sister's Fountain

North Devon

TORRIDGE DISTRICT

Parish: Welcombe
Ordnance Survey Explorer Map 126

Any pilgrimage to Devon's Holy Wells, whether on foot or by car, should properly begin, or end, at Welcombe – the valley of the well. It is the first parish in the county after leaving Cornwall's north coast at Morwenstow and it has one of the oldest and best preserved well houses. This is Atlantic coast country of wild cliffs, deep valleys and winding sunken lanes where the twisted roots of hedgerow trees are laid bare amongst a tangle of ferns, brambles and wild flowers.

In AD927 King Athleston of Wessex fixed Devon's boundary as the left bank of the River Tamar. This left a small section of land, between the source of the river at Woolley Moor and the coast, unmarked. Near here a tiny stream known as Marsland Water, flows seawards and it became the limit of the kingdom of Cornwall from Welcombe and the rest of Anglo-Saxon England. If you leave Cornwall by the unmade but public track at Gooseham, you will cross Marsland Water and be able to make your way along the old route to Welcombe church. This provides an excellent if strenuous walk, through ancient woods alive with birds, ferns and rare lichens.

The church lies about 1.5km inland from the boundary stream and nearby is the Holy Well of St Nectan. Nectan was one of the Celtic Saints who brought Christianity to Dumnonia in the period we now call the Dark Ages (and he is discussed in more detail in Chapter 3). There are legends about St Nectan associated with Rocky Valley near Tintagel in Cornwall but his most important work was in founding a community at Stoke, Hartland, just a few miles from Welcombe. This small Celtic Church community was already several hundred years old when Athleston fixed the Devon border. A number of satellite chapels were linked to the main community at Stoke; Welcombe was one of these – probably chosen because of an existing venerated spring of pure water.

1 ST NECTAN'S WELL

Grid Reference: SS228184. Good public access including for wheelchairs.

The well is situated on the roadside across the green from the parish church. The fine well-house, made from local stone, is approximately 2.5m high, has a corbelled roof and in a small niche in the gable end there is a postcard version of the holy icon of St Nectan. This shows the saint standing beside a well with the cliffs and sea in the background. The well-house is a Grade II Scheduled Monument and dates from the same 14th–15th century period as its neighbouring church. Welcombe was one of the holdings in the manor of Harton (Hartland) mentioned in King Alfred's will of AD881 and it did not become a separate parish until 1508 – a time when the well had already been a holy spot for nearly 800 years. When he visited Welcombe in the late 19th century, the Rev. Sabine Baring-Gould noted that some repairs had recently been completed on the well-house, and it is good to see it still in good order today.

A spring of clear water empties into the shallow well basin and supports water plants and ferns which in turn are home to a splendid frog which can often be seen sitting on a leaf looking like a lost prince waiting to be kissed! In the past, water from the well has been used for baptisms but there are no healing traditions now associated with it.

Traditional Uses: Baptisms.

St Nectan's Well.

Parish: Hartland
Ordnance Survey Explorer Map 126

A place of spectacular cliffs and folded rock formations dating from the Carboniferous period some 350 million years ago. A mile or so from the sea is the site of St Nectan's Celtic community which pre-dated the collegiate church founded near here in 1050 by the parents of King Harold (of Hastings fame). Their church was in turn replaced in the 12th century by the Augustinian Order of Monks who built Hartland Abbey. St Nectan's at Stoke is now the parish church of Hartland and stands on the site of the original Celtic community. It is a fine 14th century building with a 39 metre high tower – one of the tallest in Devon. A history of the parish, written in the early part of the 20th century by the local vicar, lists some fifteen ancient chapels and this confirms Hartland as being an early centre of spiritual importance.

This a parish to explore at your leisure; a visit to the Holy Wells and other places associated with St Nectan will take you along the narrow roads and ancient tracks which criss-cross an ancient landscape with its promise of spectacular views and secret coves.

2 ST NECTAN'S WELL, STOKE
Grid Reference: SS236247. Good public access by a short uneven pathway but unsuitable for wheelchairs.

Down a narrow path just a few yards from the lych-gate entrance to Stoke church, this stone built well-house is one of the most important in Devon. Legend tells us that it was to this spot that St Nectan carried his head after it had been struck off by robbers and that after he fell to the ground by the spring, his body was taken by one of the repentant attackers and buried nearby. Whatever the truth of this tale, more than one thousand five hundred years of spiritual history are concentrated in this place which is still visited by pilgrims. The well is now protected by a metal gate which prevents access to the interior but the Grade II listed building is becoming rather overgrown and the site untidy.

There is a legend that water from the well was taken and put in a pot to boil up for a feast for the local lord; the water refused to heat up and despite the fire being stoked up and more fuel added, it remained cool. On hearing of this

St Nectan's Well, Stoke.

the lord told his servants to look into the water and behold they saw a great eel swimming in the pot; the eel was quickly and carefully taken back to the well whereupon the water in the pot began to boil. The spirit of a Holy Well taking the form of an eel occurs in several folk traditions.

Traditional Uses: Baptisms.

3 BRADSTONE'S WELL, HARTLAND POINT
Grid Reference: SS224245. Good public access for those able to cope with the coast path.

A mile or so seawards from Stoke church is St Catherine's Point where a waterfall plunges down a sheer cliff to the Atlantic below; this provides a spectacular back-drop for the well which was called Bradstone's in 1760 but which is marked on the 1907 edition of the Ordnance Survey map as Brettman's Well. There are traditions of a chapel on the summit of St Catherine's Point, a swannery nearby and of a well marked by large rocks and with a stone-lined basin. A substantial stone and earth wall marks the location of the dam which formed the swannery but the well itself is now almost lost amongst the gorse and bracken which cover the hillside on the inland side of the South West Coast Path. Its presence is revealed only by a patch of damp-loving plants and the water seeping down the bank across the path on an otherwise dry hill.

Above: *Bradstone's Well.*
Above left: *St Catherine's Point.*

Bradstone's had its own rhyme:
  'If you would arise before the sun,
  And out to Bradstone's Well would run,
  Wash your eyes three times and then,
  Leave a gift and go again.'

Traditional Uses: Cure for eye problems, also for scurvy.

4 ST LEONARD'S WELL, HARTLAND
Grid Reference: SS249238. Good public access including for wheelchairs along the road from Newton Cross (leave your car here).

St Leonard's Well.

This is the site of St Leonard's Chapel one of the canon chapels linked to St Nectan's at Stoke. Remnants of stone tracery windows of medieval date are built into the wall of an old cottage which may be on the site of the original chapel building. There are traditions of a burial ground and a well associated with the chapel. Hidden amongst the ivy and undergrowth on the roadside just below a pretty thatched cottage, there are the remains of a small stone and slate structure. However, this is of probable 19th century construction and the presence of an old tap protruding from the back wall suggests that this was once the water supply for the two dwellings here. The original well is somewhere under the garden of the cottages and seems to have provided the supply of water to the tap by the roadside. A dowser has found that a stream of water passes across the whole site and does so in a complex snake-like pattern. *The Life of Saint Nectan*, written about the end of the 12th century, says that St Nectan was attacked by robbers at a place called Newtown and that he carried his head for half a league to his Holy Well; Newton Farm is close to St Leonard's Chapel. An overgrown 700-year-old lane, leads past St Leonard's and towards the direct road to St Nectan's well at Stoke. As you walk down this road you may well be retracing the saint's final journey.

Traditional Uses: Lost.

5 ST CLARE'S WELL, PHILHAM
Grid Reference: SS258226. On private land.

This well is on the site of another of the canon chapels associated with St Nectan's at Stoke and is to be found, rather neglected and overgrown, by the

St Clare's Well.

side of a busy farmyard. It has been suggested that the original dedication may have been to St Cleer, one of St Nectan's contemporaries, but the presence inside the well-house of a small relief carving of a lady (now headless) of likely 14th–15th century vintage, suggests that from an early date, a female saint was favoured. This is perhaps one of the most evocative Holy Wells in Devon with its headless figure facing out of the darkness across the now polluted water towards the light of the outside world.

Traditional Uses: Lost.

Other wells of interest in Hartland Parish:
Hartland has many early Christian sites and several of them have a tradition of a Holy Well. Possible dedications and suggested locations for some of the lost chapels are: St Mary's (Firebeacon SS245203), St James (Milford SS232225), St James (Exmansworthy SS271267), St Wenn (Christow SS250253), St Michael (Kernstone SS232237), St John (Loveland SS257264), St Heligan (South Hole SS220200), and there was also St Andrew's Well somewhere in Hartland town. An interesting survival of a butterwell (used until recent times for the cooling and storage of farm made butter) is by the roadside at Long Furlong (SS256264).

Long Furlong Well.

Parish: Clovelly
Ordnance Survey Explorer Map 126

Clovelly is adjacent to the parish of Hartland and with Woolfardisworthy West, the three parishes formed the Hundred of Hartland. The church at Clovelly was dedicated to Mary and All Saints from 1393, but this was changed to All Saints in the middle of the 18th century. No journey of exploration to this part of Devon would be complete without a visit to the picturesque village of Clovelly and to Clovelly Dykes which is a hill-fort dating from the second century BC. The cliffs at Clovelly are clothed with oakwoods which reach down to the shore and from the coast path, which runs along the top of the cliffs, you can look out across to Lundy Island where there is a tradition of at least five Holy Wells.

6 HOLIWELL
Grid Reference: SS318235. On private land.

Holiwell.

A Holiwell Farm is shown near Clovelly on modern Ordnance Survey maps. There is a well here with a shallow basin which is filled with water from a spring located in a nearby field. The lane leading to it from the farm is more than 500 years old (confirmed by a hedge-dating survey) but the well-house is of 18th–19th century construction and was used within living memory as a butterwell. Despite the name, it has not yet been possible to confirm any traditions associated with this well.

Traditional Uses: Butterwell but other traditions lost.

Parish: Woolfardisworthy
Ordnance Survey Explorer Map 126

This is one of the two places in Devon with this name (the other Woolfardisworthy parish is near Crediton – both are known in their locality as Woolsery), but we are looking here at the western parish which formed part of Hartland Hundred. The village is an Anglo-Saxon settlement and is described in the Domesday Book as being held since the Battle of Hastings by Colwin, one of the king's thegns. The church at Woolsery was linked with St Nectan's community at Stoke and was granted to Hartland Abbey at the time of Richard I. It remained a chapelry associated with the Abbey until the Reformation in the 16th century. The parish church dedication is given in early documents as Holy Trinity but since 1920 has been called All Hallows. There is an interesting legend which tells how a sailor from a ship from the Spanish Armada, which sank during a storm at nearby Buck's Mill, managed to reach as far inland as Woolsery church where he collapsed and died. The cross around his neck fell off and was found later by a vicar's daughter. An alternative explanation given for the cross is that it came from a survivor of a battle which took place in 1614 at Bitworthy near here. Unfortunately the cross went missing in 1993 and so whichever of these is the true story, it can no longer be seen.

7 LADY WELL
Grid Reference: SS334209. Good public access down a surfaced lane.

Lady Well.

Lady Well lies within sight of the church in a hedgebank which may have marked the boundary of the original Anglo-Saxon settlement. In 1984 'urgent steps' were taken by the parish authorities to check the water quality of the well and to rebuild the well-house and provide it with a padlocked door. The results of this restoration are still to be seen and perhaps it could have been done with a little more historical sensitivity. Nevertheless, it is worthy of a visit, as also is the church with its 13th century tower and its south-facing external stairway.

Traditional Uses: Good for childless couples.

Parish: Bradworthy
Ordnance Survey Explorer Map 126

The one time prosperity of Bradworthy is reflected in the large square in the centre of the village where agricultural markets were held until recent times. The parish has a number of farms and hamlets which stem from original Anglo-Saxon settlements (worthy = enclosed settlement) and the importance of the area is confirmed by the entry in the Domesday Book which values Bradworthy at £8. This is Culm grassland country which is one of Devon's most valuable habitats for wildflowers, butterflies and birds. A few herds of the native Red Ruby cattle are still to be found on the rich grazing which the areas of remaining un-reclaimed Culm provide. Exploration of the rolling landscape will repay the traveller with unspoilt countryside and quiet roads.

8   ST PETER'S WELL
Grid Reference: SS325139. Good public access but down a muddy lane.

St Peter's Well.

This little Holy Well lies in a hedgebank alongside the church of St John the Baptist; the church was dedicated to St Peter before the Reformation and the well has retained the original name. A locked metal grill protects the arched rubble stone well-house which has a water-filled basin lying just below ground level. Prior to 1859 the well was clay sided but it was then dug down to a depth of 6 feet, lined with stone, and used for some years as a public water supply. The well now seems almost to have been forgotten by local people. There are plans to develop the fields adjacent to the well and it is to be hoped that it will not be further disturbed, and perhaps the opportunity will be taken to restore it and improve access.

Traditional Uses: Lost.

9 HOLY WELL, ALFARDISWORTHY
Grid Reference: SS294118. On private land.

The farm at Alfardisworthy is close to the Cornish border and is of Anglo-Saxon origins. After 1066 it was held directly from the king by William Capra as one of three holdings in this area. It passed to the Earl of Cornwall and from 1166 until the 14th century was owned by the Tyrell family after which it went to the Cruwys family who owned it for 400 years. At the time of the Tyrells a chantry chapel was licensed for worship and the remains of this cob and stone building can still be seen just a hundred yards or so from the Holy Well. The stone well-house is set against the hedgebank of an old orchard and is fed by a number of springs which rise here; the well-house and another nearby ruined building were used for cooling butter within living memory.

Traditional Uses: Butterwell but other traditions lost.

Holy Well, Alfardisworthy.

Parish: Newton St Petroc
Ordnance Survey Explorer Map 126

The parish lies astride the A388 road and is a rural area of small fields and Culm grassland. It was given to the Priory of St Petroc of Bodmin, Cornwall, by King

St Petroc's Church.

Site of St Petroc's Well.

Athelston in AD938, a grant which was confirmed later by Henry II. The name of the parish church is St Petroc's (recorded from at least 1317) and may have arisen because of the link with the Priory. However there is a tantalising hint in the *Life of Saint Petroc* which suggests that the saint did come here in the 6th century and that events during his stay had a major influence on him.

According to legend, St Petroc was on his way back from a pilgrimage to Rome when he stopped at Newton, a place which was named for him. While he was there it rained for many days and when he was asked when the storm would end, he told the company that it would cease on the following day. However it continued to rain. The saint realised that it had been presumptuous of him to believe he could know when the rain would stop and he at once set out on a journey of penance which took him first to Rome, then to Jerusalem and on to India. He remained on his travels for seven years before returning to Britain. True or not, it is a better story than the giving of land by the king, so if it rains on your visit to Newton St Petroc, think kindly of the saint and his humility!

10 ST PETROC'S WELL
Grid Reference: SS409123. On private land.

The site of the well is now almost lost and it consists of a spring of water seeping out amongst the grass and rushes close to a field hedge some 140 metres west of the church. Formerly there were reports of a wall and stones on the site but these have all now gone or have been covered. This is one place where the disappearance of the Holy Well is of particular regret as it is directly linked by legend to the saint.

Traditional Uses: Baptisms.

Parish: Bradford and Cookbury
Ordnance Survey Explorer Map 112

In the lane which leads to the ancient church of All Saints at Bradford there is a fine old preaching cross and this is just one of the secrets which is to be found in this parish by anyone who takes the time to explore. The church at Cookbury has the unusual dedication to John the Baptist and the Seven Maccabees.

11 CADIO'S (OR FAIRY) WELL, BRADFORD

Grid Reference: SS411053. Good public access along a surfaced National Trust roadway.

This is a well to be visited with care as the traditions associated with it are concerned with ill fortune rather than with healing or good luck! It is the site where Cadio, who is mentioned in the Domesday Book as holding this manor of Dunsland from Earl Baldwin, is reported to have killed the previous Saxon owner for possession of the land. A chapel stood near the well but was demolished in the 16th century by one Humphrey Arscott who feared that he would lose his inheritance if his widowed mother went ahead with plans to remarry. A tradition of a ghostly horseman is associated with the Arscott family here.

The curse on this estate continued most recently when, after extensive renovations by the National Trust, the magnificent house on the site was completely destroyed by fire; nothing now remains apart from a small stable building and the well.

Traditional Uses: Lost.

Cadio's (or Fairy) Well, Bradford.

Holemoor Well.

12 HOLEMOOR WELL

Grid Reference: SS423057. Good access alongside a public road.

There is no reason to believe that this is other than an early source of water for the cottages grouped around the crossroads at Holemoor. However, it is worthy of inclusion and of a visit, as a good example of what a local community can do to save a small piece of its heritage. The well-house was renovated to commemorate the Millennium and it now stands close to its oak tree neighbour as a reminder of the people who lived here in the year 2000.

Traditional Uses: None known.

Parish: Holsworthy
Ordnance Survey Explorer Map 112

The unpretentious town of Holsworthy has a long history as the market centre for the surrounding agricultural districts. Its first Charter was granted in 1155 and it is still the focal point each Wednesday when the town square is filled with stalls selling local produce and goods of all descriptions. On a fine day the atmosphere is much like a provincial French market and a visit to the nearby busy cattle auction will give something of the experience which many country people still enjoy and value. Close to the town square stood a 'Great Tree' and this is where tribunals known as the Court Leet met to determine disputes about weights and measures and the quality of bread and ale. The last 'Great Tree' died at the end of the 19th century and its site is marked by a plaque set in the road.

13 ST MARY'S WELL
Grid Reference: SS343039. Good access alongside a public road.

St Mary's Well.

At the top of Victoria Hill, just a few steps from the market square and the main car park, this well is easy to find. In recent times it has been provided with a new brick enclosure and a canopy by the local Rotary Club and turned into a wishing well complete with decorative flower baskets and an old pump and trough. It stands on former glebeland and in

1882 the well was dedicated to St Mary of Trewyn (part of the town which lies close to the bottom of Victoria Hill) by the vicar, the Rev. Thornton. The reasons for this dedication have been lost.

Traditional Uses: Wishing well.

14 ST PETER'S WELL
Grid Reference: SS346038. In a garden on private land.

This site is shown on a map dated 1427 as Peter's Well Meadow and it stands close to the footpath which runs past St Peter's parish church and across the bridge over a small stream. A private house (called Petersville) was built on the land in the 1950s and at that time the well was overgrown and almost lost. In the past five years the current owner of the house and garden has cleaned up the site and erected a wishing well over the spring. He recalls that the original well was stone lined and shaped like a 'shallow bell'.

Traditional Uses: Lost.

St Peter's Well.

Other wells of interest in Holsworthy Parish:
In 1887, wells dedicated to St George and to St James were recorded in the town but no information about their location has been found. A local history written in 1934, notes that 'there is a well in the NE corner of the churchyard which was used in living memory' but this is no longer to be seen, although there are recent reports of a well being found in the yard of the old rectory next door.

Parish: Weare Giffard
Ordnance Survey Explorer Map 126

The parish takes its name from the fishing weir once to be found here; in the Domesday Book it is recorded that 'Roald pays 40d for half a fishery'. Fish were an important part of the diet when eating meat was forbidden on the many fasting days and the valuable right to take fish from rivers was subject to strict control. The river is the Torridge, famous for salmon and sea trout, and which was immortalised by Henry Williamson in his best loved book *Tarka the Otter*. Today you can use the Tarka Trail to visit the parish by bicycle or on foot.

15 TRINITY WELL
Grid Reference: SS468222. Access to the site by a level public footpath.

Site of Trinity Well.

The presence of a Holy Well here is clearly documented by an entry in the Glebe Terrier (a return of church property and lands) of 1727 which says *'there belongs to the Parish Council of Weare Giffard a well of pure water, walled and headed with stone raised walls called Trinity Well being to the north side of the highway road and adjoining to the east end of an house… where the Clerk of the Parish fetches water for Baptisms'.*

With such precise directions it should be easy to locate Trinity Well but not so; the pattern of the roads has changed and some houses have been altered or demolished. Local memories recall a well in the Glebe Field and which had the remains of an old wall around it; the field is still owned by the church and the location does fit in with the description in the Terrier. However any houses once here have gone and modern farming practices have levelled the ground and today there is nothing to be seen. A footpath along the field edge allows you to view the general site and perhaps one day some detailed work will identify the site of the 'well of pure water' which must still lie underground near here.

Traditional Uses: Baptisms.

16 CRANBURY WELL
Grid Reference: SS478221. Good access alongside a public road.

This well lies in a hedgebank alongside the road near the former Methodist Chapel built in the 19th century. It has the appearance of being used as a butterwell and as the source of water for the nearby cottages and forge which once existed here. The water is below the level of the road and the interior of the well-house is of rubble construction with evidence of plastering on some of the walls.

Cranbury Well.

Certainly not a Holy Well but worthy of a visit as a typical example of the many thousands of former water supply wells which are still marked in the Ordnance Survey maps.

Traditional Uses: Butterwell but other traditions lost.

Parish: Great Torrington
Ordnance Survey Explorer Map 126

The town of Great Torrington is one of the main inland tourist centres in this part of Devon and has managed to retain much of its character and provides good facilities for the benefit of visitors. The view across the River Torridge from the main car park is a reminder that Torrington's position made it a place of strategic importance (a Civil War battle was fought here and is still remembered as part of the town's annual celebrations).

17 COVERNEY WELL
Grid Reference: SS484197. Good public access but across uneven and in places steep ground.

Coverney Well.

This Holy Well can be difficult to find despite the fact that it is located on a popular area of common land close to the town. A short length of sunken pathway is reached from a track (known as Roman Way) which crosses Torrington Commons and this leads to a natural bowl of land surrounded by shrubs and trees; here two springs seep from the bank and a few stones mark the site of the well. It is still visited by pilgrims and there are often strips of cloth (clouties) to be found tied to the trees as marks of respect and supplication from those who have come here in search of the spirit of the place.

The name of the well is sometimes given as Covety or Coverney and both are reminiscent of the Celtic goddess of wells Coventina, who was celebrated in a Roman temple to her honour close to Hadrian's Wall in Northumbria.

Traditional Uses: Cure for eye problems.

Parish: Petrocstowe
Ordnance Survey Explorer Map 113

A Saxon chronicle called this place St Petroc's stow – the holy place of St Petroc. By the time of the Domesday Book in 1086 it was held by Buckfast Abbey (which some historians have suggested may itself have been a Celtic foundation). Ownership by the abbey was confirmed by the Bishop of Exeter in 1150 and the abbot was responsible for appointing the parish priest here until the Reformation. Such an ancient Christian foundation might be expected to have a Holy Well and there are indeed a number of springs and wells in the old lane which comes down over the hill to the church. Any local tradition for a Holy Well has been lost however except for comments that the wells have 'always been here and never fail'.

18 LANE WELL
Grid Reference: SS513092. Public access along the lane which provides good walking.

Adjacent to the lane and in front of some old cottages there is a stone and brick well-house set into the bank. It has been used in the past as a supply of drinking water and the owner recalls that, in his youth, each year the inside of the well-house was lime-washed and a bag of lime was sunk into the 2-metre deep water to purify it. A number of other springs and wells are to be found in the lane.

Traditional Uses: Water supply but other traditions lost.

Parish: Halwill
Ordnance Survey Explorer Map 112

Since Saxon times this parish has taken its name from the Holy Well – Halgewella.

It is now an area of fields and forestry plantations which provide a variety of safe off-road walks and for which the Information Centre at Cookworthy Moor is an excellent base. Halwill village is off the main A3079 road and worthy of a visit to see the stump of a preaching cross in the churchyard; these crosses were used as gathering points and may have been used before a permanent church building was completed.

Above: *Lane Well.*
Above left: *Ancient lane to St Petroc's Church.*

Above: *Halwill church cross.*
Right: *Chapel Holy Well.*

The Rev. Sabine Baring-Gould visited here in the late 19th century and noted that *'a well from which this place is named, still exists with the ruins of a chapel nearby'.*

19 CHAPEL HOLY WELL
Grid Reference: SS438001. On private land.

This Holy Well has appeared in so many historical documents and gave its name to the settlement, and yet is difficult to find. Across the fields from the parish church of St Peter and close to the main road is the site of Chapel Farm and a recent housing development called Holywell Close. Behind the new development, a small stream runs through a tangled patch of scrubland and past a ruined brick building which may have once been a pump house; an elderly lady who lived in the parish all her days reported that she can remember as a girl that water from the well under this ruin was used for baptisms.

It seems that this is all that remains of the Halgewella of Domesday, a place which was used long before the Normans and perhaps even before the Saxons came across the moors and wetlands of Dumnonia. Sad indeed.

Traditional Uses: Baptisms.

Other Parishes:
There are some other places in Torridge District where there are traditions of a Holy Well or references to wells of ancient lineage. These include:
Abbotsham – durnawille – 'the hidden spring' NW of Cockington Farm; mentioned in a boundary agreement 1154.
Beaford – Holy Well at Holy Orchard near Abbots Hill Farm.
Broadwoodwidger – Slew Wood Wells.
Shebbear – Holy Well – place name in document dated 1322.

WEST DEVON DISTRICT

Parish: Hatherleigh
Ordnance Survey Explorer Map 113

Hatherleigh means a clearing or glade in the hawthorn wood. By 1086 the manor together with 'kerswell' the cress-spring, was held by the Abbot of Tavistock. Today it is on the Tarka Trail and the West Devon Sticklepath cycle route. The town with its weekly cattle market, thatched buildings and Town Trail, is a delight to visit. The monument just outside the town and overlooking Hatherleigh Common, commemorates a local man who distinguished himself at the Charge of the Light Brigade in 1854 and is most useful for the view it provides of northern Dartmoor and of High Willhays, the highest point on the moor (2037 feet).

20 ST JOHN'S WELL
Grid Reference: SS552044. Situated just a short way off the Tarka Trail where it crosses the Common, this well has good public access for those able to manage normal field walking.

The attractive little brick well-house is located in a small hollow of rough scrub growth and the whole site is damp from the springs which rise here; it may be the 'kerswell' once owned by the Abbot of Tavistock. There has been some recent restoration work on the well.

St John's Well.

The parish church is dedicated to John the Baptist but prior to the Reformation had a double dedication to Mary and John, and this earlier dedication accounts for the names of the two Holy Wells in this parish.

Traditional Uses: Baptisms.

21 ST MARY'S WELL
Grid Reference: SS523058. On private land.

Lost in woodland, there is now little to see except for a spring seeping into a shallow natural basin and water trickling away through some moss-covered stones. However this place does have a special atmosphere and it was once the destination for processions and revels on Ascension Day and Holy Thursday. It was used for fortune telling when pins would be dropped into the water and a wish quietly whispered; until recently offerings of flowers and clouties were left by the well.

Traditional Uses: Wishing well.

St Mary's Well.

Parishes: Coryton and Lewtrenchard
Ordnance Survey Explorer Map 112

'The scenery in this locality is beautiful with well wooded hills, lovely vales and a gently meandering river (the latter well stocked with trout).'
Kelly's Directory of 1866

The two small neighbouring parishes of Coryton and Lewtrenchard are tucked away in rural West Devon in a secret landscape where it comes as no surprise to find a tradition of ancient, holy sites. They each have a Holy Well dedicated to a Celtic saint, close to a parish church standing on ground where there has been a sacred building since recorded history.

Coryton seems to take its name from St Curig who was one of that band of notable men and women who travelled throughout Ireland, Wales and the Westcountry during the 6th and early 7th centuries founding small communities of Christians. He went on to become a Bishop in Brittany before returning to Wales. After his death in AD550, his silver bishop's staff was claimed to have healing properties (in much the same way as the water of many Holy Wells is believed to have curative or fortune telling powers).

We do not know whether St Curig did come to Coryton. However the link with him was established from an early date and an Anglo-Saxon missal refers to this area as Corigton or LlanCurig; the word Llan (Old Welsh or possibly Old Cornish Lann) usually refers to a place associated with a sacred site. The association with St Curig lives on in the parish name (Coriton in the Domesday Book), although any direct linkage was lost in September 1261 when the church building then on the site was re-dedicated by Bishop Branscombe and placed under the patronage of St Andrew.

The next parish is Lewtrenchard where association with St Petroc has a long tradition. The connection may have arisen from a visit by that foremost of Cornish Saints who we know travelled throughout Western Britain (and according to some histories of his life, to Rome, Jerusalem and even India). Or it may be that laying claim to his name was a way for the local people in former times to identify with the powerful Celtic Priory of St Petroc at Bodmin – in much the same way that local firms today attach the name 'Duchy' to their goods to signal some special quality or value. Whatever the real reason, the tradition of St Petroc at Lewtrenchard is well established.

The dedication of a sacred place to St Petroc is another association which was lost when an enlarged building here was re-consecrated by Bishop Branscombe (him again!) in 1261. Since at least the 18th century, the parish church has been known as St Peter's. Despite this, the tradition of St Petroc and a Holy Well close to the church has persisted.

22 ST CURIG'S WELL, CORYTON
Grid Reference: SX456836. Good public access as the well is alongside a road.

A well is to be found alongside the road only 150m away from the gate which leads behind some old cottages, and along a narrow leafy pathway to the attractive church of St Andrew. It is an open-fronted, stone built well-house approximately 1m high and 1.5m wide with a flat slate as a roof. It is a drip-

St Curig's Well, Coryton.

Bate Farm.

ping well with a shallow, water-and-mud-filled basin and it is set into the roadside hedge which a dating survey confirmed to be at least 500 years old. An 18th century map shows that there were some cottages in the field immediately behind this hedge and it is possible that the well here was the water supply to these dwellings.

According to some local traditions, the real Holy Well of St Curig was on the lower side of the road immediately opposite the church, where there is now a gateway to Bate Farm.

The present occupier has confirmed that many years ago there was a spring of water here but it was filled in and the water piped away. So the search for St Curig's well remains inconclusive.

Traditional Uses: Lost.

23 ST PETROC'S WELL, LEWTRENCHARD
Grid Reference: SX459861. Good level access to the well which is in the grounds of a hotel.

Above: *Lew copse.*
Right: *St Petroc's Well.*

Lewtrenchard provides a good example of how, despite the centuries during which such places have been powerful spiritual symbols of Christian traditions, Holy Wells can be neglected and then forgotten. As late as 1830, the curate of the parish, Mr Caddy-Thomas, noted that 'the Holy Well behind the church has been re-erected and formerly its water was used for the font.' But by 1964 it was noted by a local historian only that 'there is a possibility of a Holy Well in the copse above the church.' More recent local enquiries including a conversation with a long-time resident and member of the church, did not produce any knowledge about such a well. A search of the copse which adjoins the way-marked Tarka Trail, revealed only a rather startled fox and a jumble of old walls, drainage ditches and channels. There is also a complex of springs and water catchment pits which serve the nearby barns and fields, and the site of the Holy Well is now lost amongst these.

However there is a fine St Petroc's Well at Lewtrenchard, albeit a product of more modern romanticism. Between 1881 and 1924 the eminent hymn writer, collector of folk traditions and recorder of British Saints, Sabine Baring-Gould, was the squire and parson here, and it was his influence which resurrected the link with St Petroc. His enthusiasm led him to have a 'Holy Well' built in the grounds of his house (now the Lewtrenchard Manor Hotel) close to the ornamental pond he also laid out. It is Baring-Gould's St Petroc's well which is included in the official register of Grade II Listed Monuments for Devon where it is described as 'a small rectangular well-house with a corbelled granite roof and chamfered round-headed doorway below a simple round headed niche with a stone cross in the gable'.

Although this may not be a site of real antiquity, Baring-Gould included some of the original well stones in his construction (just as the Duke of Bedford had done when he moved a Holy Well into his gardens at nearby Endsleigh).

Traditional Uses: Baptisms.

A visit to Lewtrenchard church, to Baring-Gould's St Petroc's Holy Well, to nearby Lew Mill with its ancient stone monolith and adjacent Elizabethan Dower House, and then walks along the surrounding network of footpaths, will do much to capture something of the feeling of kinship with the natural world which is our heritage from the Celtic Saints.

Parish: Okehampton
Ordnance Survey Explorer Map 113

Okehampton is an ancient town whose character was much changed by heavy traffic during the middle decades of the last century, but it is now regaining some of its former glory. The ruins of a splendid Norman castle are a reminder that this was the seat of the High Sheriff of Devon and of the importance once attached to control over the strategic crossing of the River Okement and the northern route around Dartmoor. The town makes an excellent base for an itinerary of visits to a number of Holy Wells in the surrounding countryside.

24 FITZ'S WELL
Grid Reference: SX592937. Good public access, situated on Dartmoor but very close to a road and on open ground.

This well is near the military camp just outside Okehampton and is clearly marked by an ancient Dartmoor Cross almost a metre in height. The spring itself is covered by massive granite slabs and a metal cover. A number of rags and ribbons are often to be seen tied to a nearby tree which shows that this Holy Well is still visited by those concerned about their health and fortune.

The cross may have come from a chapel dedicated to St Michael which once stood nearby at Halstock. A local legend tells how a man and his wife who had been worshipping at the chapel, got lost on the moor and became convinced that they had been put under a spell which could only be broken if they could find a spring of pure water. They came across this spring and found their way home and afterwards they had the cross erected in thanksgiving. In 1676 the spring at Fitz's Well was said to have run dry but it was soon noted that cattle were again using it as a watering place; water a plenty now runs from the spring. Until late in the 19th century, the tradition was for young people to visit the well on Easter morning to learn their fortune. The well is credited to Sir John Fitz who also built another near Princetown (Well 28).

Traditional Uses: Wishing well and general healing.

Parishes: Belstone and Sticklepath
Ordnance Survey Explorer Map 113

Just a few miles from Okehampton along the B3260 road (this is the old A30), the village of Belstone stands overlooking the moor and the headwaters of the River Taw which flows from here to the sea at Barnstaple. This is a true moorland settlement with a cattle pound, village stocks and 13th-century granite

Fitz's Well.

church which has been dedicated to St Mary since 1846 (the original dedication is unknown). A large stone leans against the church wall and on it is a rough carving of a cross in a circle; this is probably a very early Christian horizontal tomb cover. This tomb and the stone circle (3000 years older) on the slopes of Belstone Common, are reminders that Belstone has been a place of spirituality since these moors were first settled.

Sticklepath is a village a couple of miles further along the old A30 road from Belstone (and strictly speaking it falls into the parish of Sampford Courtenay). It is a village with a long history connected to the harnessing of water power and at one time there were at least seven water-wheels at work producing power for various small workshops. In the 18th century, a number of Quaker families established a woollen and cloth-making business here. The site of the woollen mill was later taken over by the Finch family who ran a thriving iron foundry and agricultural tool manufacturing enterprise from 1814 at the very start of the Industrial Revolution, until 1960. The Finch Foundry still exists and today the original water-powered drop-hammers and tool making machines are under the guardianship of the National Trust.

Tom Pearse, owner of the 'old grey mare' which went to Widecombe Fair in the traditional song, is buried in the old Quaker Burial Ground behind the Finch Foundry.

25 HOLY WELL, BELSTONE
Grid Reference: SX620935. Good public access just a little way on to the moor close to the road below the church.

On the sloping moorland grass and within a few hundred yards of the church, close to the well-worn path which leads down and on to the moor proper, some large granite slabs form a small well-house above a tiny spring. Sheep and cattle use it for drinking and the stones as a rubbing post. In the past the

Holy Well, Belstone.

well has been used as a supply of drinking water for nearby cottages and it also had a reputation for curative powers.

From here there are splendid walks on the moor and, for those who are able to travel over rough ground, a particular trail will take you along the river through the ferns and bracken of Belstone Cleave to the next Holy Well at Sticklepath.

Traditional Uses: General healing.

26 LADY WELL, STICKLEPATH
Grid Reference: SX639942. Good public access, the well is by the roadside.

As the road dips down into the village, Lady Well is to be found on the right-hand verge. A little stone structure has a lintel with the words 'LADY WELL DRINK AND BE THANKFUL' carved into it; an instruction which many weary travellers in times past must have been pleased to follow. A small stone trough still receives water from a pipe jutting from the stones. A few yards up the hill behind the well is an ancient standing stone with a cross carved in relief on its western face.

Traditional Uses: Lost.

Lady Well, Sticklepath.

Parish: Sampford Courtenay
Ordnance Survey Explorer Map 113

Just a few miles to the north of Sticklepath lies the village of Sampford Courtenay. This is where a final act in the struggle by the people of Dumnonia to retain some of their religious identity was played out. In 1549 changes were made to church services and a new Prayer Book was introduced. Services were to be said in English and not in Latin and many of the old rituals were changed. The Cornish in particular were disturbed by these proposals, many of the people in the West did not speak English and they were comfortable with the familiar Latin phrases. They became further aggrieved when attempts were made to remove traditional statues from their churches. A Cornish 'army' made a start for London to try and persuade the king to restore the old form of services.

At Sampford Courtenay, local people were also alarmed at the alterations made to the services in their parish church of St Andrew and matters came to a head here on Whit Sunday 1549 when a landowner, who spoke up for the changes, was murdered in front of the Church House. The Devon villagers joined the Cornishmen on their march; the Prayer Book Rebellion, as it became to be known, had begun.

The four thousand strong army of 'Commoners of Devonshyre and Cornwall' as they called themselves, besieged Exeter where they drew up a petition which rejected the new service in English 'because it is but lyke a Christmas game' and asked for the restoration of the Latin Mass and all ancient rites; in addition the petition said 'we wyll that the halfe parte of the abbey landes and chantrye landes, in euerye mans possessions, how so euer he cam by them, be geuen again to two places, where two of the chief Abbeia was in euery Countye…'. In effect they were asking for some of the lands taken by the king at the Dissolution of the Monasteries to be given back. Their progress was halted when they were defeated by the king's forces at Fenny Bridges near Honiton. The Devon and Cornish army retreated and on 17 August 1549 at Greenhill, Sampford Courtenay, it was again engaged by forces loyal to the king. Hundreds were killed and the Prayer Book Rebellion was squashed.

It is interesting to note that forces who fought for the king were largely foreign mercenaries commanded by one John Russell, later Duke of Bedford, the man who had been given the lands of both Tavistock and Dunkeswell Abbeys at the Dissolution. This was the last time in which the people from the old Celtic Kingdom of Dumnonia fought together in a local movement in defence of their religious freedoms.

27 PARISH WELL

Grid Reference: SS634013. Public access through the churchyard or along a side path.

Next to the church is Church House, where the murder took place in 1549; beside it there is a gate which leads down the 'water lane' and around the back of the churchyard. Almost directly behind the church tower, and down a bank which slopes away from the cemetery, are a few large granite stones which mark the site of the Holy Well. A trickle of water runs into the dense growth of brambles, nettles and ivy and these few half-buried stones are all that

Parish Well.

St Andrew's church from Parish Well.

remains of the well which was here from very early times and which would have provided water for those fighting for their religion in 1549.

Up to about fifty years ago the well was kept clear and clean but now rubbish and grass clippings from the churchyard are being tipped down the bank and have almost buried the well.

Traditional Uses: Lost.

Parish: Lydford
Ordnance Survey Explorer Map OL28

Much of Dartmoor lies in the parish of Lydford which takes its name from the settlement established by the Anglo-Saxons near a fording place over the river. It became a place of some importance and soon after taking control of this part of Devon, the king set up a mint for coinage. The *Anglo-Saxon Chronicle* records that in AD997 Lydford was sacked by Vikings who made their way up the River Tamar and across country 'burning or killing each thing that they met'. After Lydford, the Vikings returned to their longships via Tavistock where they burnt down the newly-established abbey.

The parish church of St Petroc stands in the village next to the site of a castle keep which became the prison used by the Stannary Courts who were responsible for overseeing every aspect of mining, smelting and refining tin from the workings which existed at various places on the moor since very early times. The conditions in the dungeons at Lydford were harsh and reported to be the worst in the kingdom.

28 FICE'S WELL
Grid Reference: SX578759. A public footpath to this well is signposted off the B3257 road near the junction to Princetown and it provides easy walking across the fields (apart from the last 50 yards or so where it becomes a little boggy and overgrown).

Although it is in Lydford parish, Fice's Well is some miles from the village and is much closer to Princetown and H.M. Prison, Dartmoor. It is on land which was reclaimed from the moor and enclosed by prison authorities but the well

Fice's Well.

was here long before then and was built by the same Fitz family who also built the wells at Okehampton (Well 24) and at Tavistock (Well 31). It is an attractive structure of granite blocks and with the inscription 'I F 1568' carved above the entrance; a moorstone wall built by convicts in the 19th century surrounds it and the enclosure provides an ideal habitat for wildflowers such as ragged robin and moor grasses.

The Rev. S. Baring-Gould came here in the 19th century and on that occasion some of his party, including officers from the Ordnance Survey complete with surveying equipment, went astray in the mist and became completely lost. Baring-Gould notes that this was a case of people being 'pixie-led out of pure mischief to show how superior the pixies were even to the most scientific equipment'.

Traditional Uses: Lost.

Parish: Tavistock
Ordnance Survey Explorer Map 108

Tavistock has all the features which are desirable in a small market town, interesting buildings, an ancient church, a varied market, excellent local shops and places for refreshment. Its prosperity in the Middle Ages owed much to the wool trade and to the influence of the abbey, and later to the Dukes of Bedford who held vast mineral rights in the area and who re-invested some of the great wealth, earned from their tin and copper mines, in remodelling the town in the 18th and 19th centuries. The relationship of the Bedfords with Tavistock stems from the Dissolution of the Monasteries in 1539 when the king granted many of the properties taken from Tavistock Abbey (and from Dunkeswell Abbey in East Devon) to John Russell, who became the first duke.

Today only a few remnants of the abbey buildings remain and they can be seen around the centre of the town. However, in the Middle Ages the abbey was one of the great monastic houses of Devon. It had ten altars at which the sacristan said prayers, and an ornate and richly-decorated sanctuary containing the bones of St Rumon; it owned lands and property in many parts of the county. The town makes an excellent centre to discover some of the Holy Wells in this part of Devon.

29 ST JOHN'S WELL
Grid Reference: SX479739. Excellent public access along a surfaced path from the town centre.

St John's Well.

On the opposite bank of the River Tavy from the site of Tavistock Abbey there is a pathway close to the river; this path is bounded by a high bank and about half way along its length (near a convenient street light post) is St John's Holy Well. A fine carved granite canopy is set into the bank and it protects the well which consists of a dripping wall and a small basin of stones. In 1946 a broken cross was located next to the well but this has gone, possibly moved when improvement works were carried out a decade or so later.

The well marks the place where a small chapel was used by John the Hermit who is recorded as being here in 1470 and who may have been a member of a noble family and seeking spiritual retreat. John was clearly not an impoverished monk as it is recorded in a document of 1535 that John the Hermit (John Armytt) had left a 'little cross of silver in which is a piece of the True Cross' to the abbey.

Within living memory, it was considered good luck to throw a pebble over your left shoulder into St John's Holy Well.

Traditional Uses: Wishing well.

St John's Well, capstone.

30 WEST STREET WELL
   Grid Reference: SX479745. Good public access; in a hotel conservatory.

West Street Well.

Tavistock Abbey was founded in AD974 at a place which was not too close to the River Tamar which was the boundary between Devon and Cornwall, but sufficiently near it so that the abbot's influence would be felt in Cornwall where the Celtic Church tradition was still strong. The choice of Tavistock was said to have been due to a vision experienced by Ordulf, its Anglo-Saxon founder, but his reason was more likely because of the presence of an existing Christian community. Evidence for this comes from a 6th century inscribed memorial stone found here; such memorials are Christian in origin and were erected close to a church or cemetery. Further support for an existing Christian community in Tavistock comes in King Ethelred's Charter of AD981, which confirmed the establishment of the Abbey of St Mary and St Rumon, and which alludes to an existing abbot; the monks believed that a small chapel, which seems to have been located near the area which is now West Street, was older than the abbey itself.

A lease of 1597 by Charles Grylls and Thomas Llybbe includes reference to a well close to the garden and tenement in West Street, once held by William Venton. In 2000 during refurbishment of an old inn, this well was uncovered and restored. It is now a feature in the floor of the conservatory of Brown's Hotel; the water still runs clear and pure and is sold bottled in the hotel bar! An ancient well with links to Tavistock's very early Christian heritage is restored to use.

Traditional Uses: Lost.

31 FITZ'S WELL
Grid Reference: SX474739. Good public access, the well is in a small grassy area beside a road.

Fitz's Well.

Tavistock's third well is located at Boughthayes which is a road opposite the Catholic church on Callington Road. Its origins can be traced back to the same Fitz family who are also associated with the wells at Okehampton (Well 24) and at Lydford (Well 28).

In 1568, John Fitz was granted a lease by eight local men and churchwardens 'to digge and make a trench any waie thorowe the garden as well as to laie therin pipes of tymbre, lydd or otherwise to carry water in the same from one fountene or spring lyinge and being in the close of the said John fftyz called boughthayes into the mansion house of said John ffytz.'

John Fitz at that time occupied the farm and large house known as Fitzford House and for which now only the gatehouse remains standing near Drake's statue. There is a legend of a ghostly carriage which each midnight, takes the lady of the manor from Fitzford House to Okehampton Castle where a hound plucks a blade of grass – a journey she is cursed to make, until every blade of grass has gone from the Castle Green, in atonement for the murder of four husbands. The well-house at Boughthayes is a square, stone building with a fine granite door frame and lintel and with a slate plaque over the door (vandalised) bearing the Fitz coat of arms. The building has been restored on a number of occasions but is subject to continuing vandalism and neglect; the 'fountene or spring' inside is now filled with rubbish.

Traditional Uses: None known.

Parishes: Lifton and Bradstone
Ordnance Survey Explorer Map 112

Lifton is familiar to all those who travelled by road to Cornwall before the construction of the new A30 road which bypassed Okehampton and Launceston. Today the thundering lines of traffic have gone, and a drive along the old road (now called the West Devon Way) provides a chance to enjoy the scenery and places along the way. Lifton has regained some peace but it also had its times of splendour and importance. It was a royal holding and was the centre of Lifton Hundred where the court of Anglo-Saxon Kings had met.

Plaque of Fitz coat of arms.

Carved head, St Nonna's Church, Bradstone.

Its tiny next-door neighbour Bradstone is easy to overlook. There is no village and most travellers between Tavistock and Launceston are hurrying to cross into Cornwall over the River Tamar at Greystone Bridge and do not turn down the narrow road which leads to this rural backwater. But Bradstone should not be missed by anyone who has an interest in the history of Devon, it has a number of secrets to delight. The most striking is the gatehouse at Bradstone Barton; this early 17th-century building has features which are unique in Devon. As you walk along the road from the

church it is a most impressive sight and gives a feeling of stepping into history. Bradstone was already an important place in Saxon times and in 1050 manumission to free two slaves – Byrhflaed of Trematon and Aeflaed of Stoke Climsland – was issued from here by a visiting nobleman who fell ill and who no doubt hoped this act of mercy would secure his recovery. Another secret is the 12th-century church of St Nonna which is no longer used for worship and is in the care of the Churches Conservation Trust. It is a building of simple style to which an air of mystery is added by a stone carving of a man's head which stares down across the church from a wall on one side of the altar.

Above: *Parish pump well, Lifton.*
Right: *Holy Well, Lifton.*

32 HOLY WELL, LIFTON

Grid Reference: SX389848. Good public access via a public footpath or for those unable to walk through the field, it can be reached by the road near old Lifton Bridge.

Next to the gateway into the churchyard of St Andrew's Church at Lifton there is a bricked up wellhouse. Although this might be taken as the site of the Holy Well, it is in fact the site of the 19th-century parish pump which supplied water to the village before the coming of a mains water supply. Nevertheless it is an interesting feature and worthy of a second glance before walking on to the site of the real Holy Well.

In 1898 the Rev. Sabine Baring-Gould noted that 'at Lifton below Donce Hill is a never failing well, the Holy Well from which until within a few years, the water was always fetched for baptisms. Lately this path has been stopped; it is not five minutes from the church.' Fortunately the path is now opened and signposted and takes you from the road at the side of the church through a field, down a flight of steps and towards Lifton Bridge. A few yards after the steps, the stone wall of the lodge building will be found and water from the Holy Well spring empties into the gully from an old granite chute.

Traditional Uses: Baptisms.

33 ST NONNA'S WELL, BRADSTONE
Grid Reference: SX382807. Good public access; by the roadside.

In 1899 the Rev. Baring-Gould wrote 'a former rector of Bradstone told me that the unfailing spring on the Glebe was used for christening'. Today that spring is still there, approached by an old cobbled path and in the curve of a wall; unfortunately the well itself has recently been badly damaged by landscaping works. The stone roofing slab is undamaged and the owner of the site hopes to renovate the well area to the condition it was in when it was in use by the local cottagers as a source of water and a butterwell.

Above: *St Nonna's Well.*
Left: *St Nonna's Church from the well.*

St Nonna was the mother of St David of Wales and she is remembered with church dedications not only in Wales but also in Brittany and Cornwall. Bradstone is a few miles from the important church of Altarnun in Cornwall which is dedicated to St Nonna and where there was a Holy Well famous for its cures for the insane. The saint is known to have visited this area of Dumnonia where her sister (St Wenn) lived. There are some doubts about the original dedication of the church at Bradstone; St Christopher and St Matthias are the other suggested patrons here. The medieval dedication is not documented and it is entirely reasonable to accept the local tradition of identifying this church and Holy Well with St Nonna.

Traditional Uses: Baptisms.

Parishes: Thrushelton and Stowford
Ordnance Survey Explorer Map 112

If you want to feel what it was like to live in Devon during the Middle Ages then park your car at Lewdown on the West Devon Way road, take a stout stick in your hand, throw a pack over your shoulder and walk along the narrow lanes and the footpaths which take you to Thrushelton and on to Stowford. You may meet mud in plenty but also a countryside of wildflowers and birdsong, and as you approach the church of St George at Thrushelton, tucked away next to its tiny (and a bit run-down church house), it would come as no real surprise to see ahead of you a herd of scraggy cattle being herded by a drover who had stepped straight out of a 15th-century woodcut. At Stowford there are thatched houses from Tudor times and an ancient bridge where the ford marked by staves (and which gave the village its name), once crossed the River Thrushel. A Stowford Parish Trail leaflet provides an excellent description of the history of this parish, and of the ill fortune which has become attached to a particular field where there have been three tragic deaths in the past 200 years. On returning to your car, take note of the Harris Arms which is the only pub in Devon which displays a motto in the Cornish language: 'Car Dew dres pub tra' (Love God above everything). The Harris family brought their motto with them when they moved from Penzance to Hayne Manor, Stowford, many hundreds of years ago when Cornish was still spoken in the far west of the old kingdom of Dumnonia.

34 DRINKING TROUGH SPRING
Grid Reference: SX433870. Good public access; the spring is by the roadside.

Stowford is a Celtic Christian site and near the churchyard gate stands one of the few 5th–6th century memorial stones which remain in Devon (this is discussed in more detail in Chapter 3). One theory about the stone is that it is in some way connected to St Curig of nearby Coryton (Well 22), and although there is no evidence to support this, it is true that the first dedication of the church in that parish is unknown (John the Baptist since 1883). This might indicate a Celtic Saint as the original patron. Set into the roadside wall a few yards from the memorial stone, there is a small stone and slate structure and into which flows a plentiful supply of spring water. This seems to be a drinking trough of probable 18th–19th century construction, and no doubt in former times was used to water the horses of the more affluent members of the church congregation. No claim is made for it as a Holy Well but a plentiful spring of pure water so close to an ancient Celtic site is at least worthy of note.

Traditional Uses: None known.

Drinking Trough Spring.

Parish: Bere Ferrers
Ordnance Survey Explorer Map 108

The Bere Peninsula is aptly named, as less than a mile of dry land separates the River Tamar and the River Tavy at Broadwell, near the point where the single road runs in and out of this parish. Centuries of exploitation of silver, tin and copper mines once provided employment for the hundreds of miners and engineers who lived in the villages of Bere Alston and Bere Ferrers, but the scars of the industrial landscape have healed. This is Devon, but Cornwall is just across the mudflats of the tidal River Tamar, and there was an ancient ferry route between Thorn Point and Cargreen which operated within living memory. A network of narrow roads and paths criss-cross the parish, passing the remnants of old apple, cherry and plum orchards and flower fields for which the Bere Peninsula was once renowned.

35 HALLOWELL
Grid Reference: SX466641. Good public access; well by the roadside.

The signpost to Hallowell suggests the presence of a Holy Well. Close to the site of an old quay at Gnatham on the River Tavy, there is a tiny well-house built into the bank of Hallowell Wood. The wood was once owned by the monks of Buckland Abbey who also had salmon fishing rights in the river (in 1280 a bitter dispute about these rights with the monks of Tavistock Abbey, led to a servant being shot in the arm by an arrow).

Right: *Hallowell.*
Below: *Bere Ferrers.*

Behind the locked door of the well-house, there is a dripping wall where water falls into a small natural-stone basin. This present well-house was built in the mid-1990s to replace an older stone structure which had become a hazard.

Despite the promise of the name, the recent discovery of a document from 1450 casts some doubt over the true origins of this well. The new evidence comes from an itinerary of a parish priest which lists all the main places around Bere Ferrers, either as a record of his progress to take communion around the parish or the order in which parishioners would attend Mass on holy days. The site of the well is given in this itinerary but as Aller-wylle (the alder well) and not Halla-wylle (the Holy Well).

The confusion about the place name is further compounded by a 19th-century record which identifies a Holy Well 'under the churchyard wall' at Bere Ferrers and with the curious name 'Basil Well'. This may be a reference to an important saint of that name who introduced monasticism to Asia Minor. There is no local knowledge of such a well.

Traditional Uses: None known.

Parish: Sheepstor
Ordnance Survey Explorer Map OL28

This is a typical moorland parish of scattered farms and a few houses grouped around the 15th-century church of St Leonard; today fewer than one hundred people live here. The story of Sheepstor is one of sheep and cattle farming but also of a tin mining community. In 1168 Guy de Bretteville was fined three marks 'for his men of Sheepstor (Siltelestorre) because they have dug for tin in the King's Forest (Dartmoor) against the rules,' which probably meant they had been doing so without first staking a claim with the Stannary Courts. It was not always a peaceful place; near the church gate is the spot where the cruel sport of bull baiting was once carried out. The ring, to which a bull would be tied before a pack of dogs was set on it, is still there sunk in the ground.

Sheepstor was the home of the White Rajahs of Sarawak and the tombs of Sir James Brooke, the first White Rajah, and of his heirs to that title, Sir Charles Brooke and Sir Vyner Brooke, are in the churchyard, together with that of Bertram Brooke, the Tuan Muda – the Young Lord. The remarkable story of that family's links with far away Sarawak is recorded in the church.

36 ST LEONARD'S WELL
    Grid Reference: SX561676. Good public access; well is by the roadside.

Through the back of the churchyard and beside the road to the moor is the pretty little Holy Well. The spring which feeds the well is ancient and has always existed close to where the church now stands; it is mentioned in a deed of 1570. However the present well-house is not in the original location. The spring was on land purchased in about 1875 for the Glebe to support a parson in the parish; some 30 years after this, the then incumbent seems to have become concerned about the number of people crossing his land to reach the well. A scheme was designed to pipe the water from the spring across the land to a new well-house on the roadside. This was built from stone tracery taken from the church windows during restoration in the 1850s. So St Leonard's Well is built of ancient stones and the water is from the original spring, but its location is Victorian.

Traditional Uses: Lost.

St Leonard's Well.

Parish: Chagford
Ordnance Survey Explorer Map OL28

Another of Devon's Stannary towns. Today it is a delightful base from which to explore the fringes of the moor. Castle Drogo near here is sometimes called the last castle built in England, and its position overlooking the steep wooded slopes of the River Teign is very suggestive of a medieval defensive site. This National Trust property only dates from the last century but it is impressive and so too is the much smaller burial chamber at Spinster's Rock, a couple of miles away, which is more than 3000 years older than Castle Drogo. This is an area where careful study of the Ordnance Survey map will reveal much of interest, including Chagford Bridge, Gidleigh Castle and the standing stones and stone rows on Chagford Common.

37 DRUID'S WELL
Grid Reference: SX716861. Good public access; the well is by the roadside.

Above: *Druid's Well.*
Right: *Middlecott Cross.*

The name supports the appearance of this well as the massive moss-covered granite slabs look as if they have stood here for ever. However this may not be for much longer as a recent collision with a vehicle has shifted the stones to the extent that they now look in danger of collapse, and the spring which they protect is choked with mud and debris. The site is next to Middlecott which was a Domesday settlement and close by are two ancient stone crosses known as Middlecott Cross and Week Down Cross. These are early Christian monuments dating from 7th–9th centuries and suggest that a route across the moor once ran through here.

Ancient stones in this part of Devon have not always been treated carefully, one of the crosses was once taken down and used as a bridge over a stream and the other was put into service as the foundation of a farm water pump; perhaps the stones of Druid's Well will receive better treatment.

Traditional Uses: Lost.

Other Parishes:
Other places in West Devon where there are traditions of a Holy Well or references to wells of ancient lineage include:
Milton Abbot – Holy Well in the grounds of Endsleigh House. This was moved here by the Duke of Bedford in 1814 as a decorative feature; it came from Leigh Barton Farm nearby – St Leonard's Well; tradition of a well and remains of an ancient chapel – Dunterton; a document of 1793 suggests there was a well near here associated with an ancient chapel.
North Tawton – Bathe Pool; a natural pool which fills to forecast national disaster.
Princetown – Clazywell; a dark supposedly bottomless pool associated with a witch but actually formed by the subsidence of a 17th-century tin working.
Walkhampton – reference to a Roger de Halghewille in 1333 and place name Holwell.
Whitchurch – place name Holwell House which was the seat of the Glanville family for 300 years.

GREATER PLYMOUTH AND SOUTH HAMS DISTRICT

Above: *Finewell Street.*
Right: *Buckwell Street.*

Parish: Greater Plymouth
Ordnance Survey Explorer Map 108

The City of Plymouth is one of the main centres of Devon. It has a long history as a commercial and fishing port, as a naval base, and as an excellent place to shop and to visit. Attractions include the National Marine Aquarium (good for wet days), and the historic Barbican area by the fishing quays. Even before the devastating bombing of the Second World War, the city had expanded beyond the boundaries of the original waterside settlement and today it extends into the hinterland along the estuaries of the rivers Plym and Tamar. During the Roman era, a port and trading centre flourished around the Mount Batten area and by the 8th century a priory was in existence at the head of the Plym estuary (it was closed in 1121 because of the unseemly behaviour of the monks, but was then re-founded to become one of the richest Augustinian monastic houses in England). A hospital for lepers was set up nearby in 1307. At this time, Sutton Pool was the focus for sea traders and a military base.

Early religious centres in the area include St Budeaux, where the Celtic Saint St Budoc is claimed to have landed. This, like the medieval manors of Hooe, Goosewell, Langage, Egg Buckland and Staddiscombe, has now been absorbed by the growth of the city. A number of traditions speak of Holy Wells in the Greater Plymouth area, but today there is little evidence of these to be found beyond street names.

38 ST EDMUND'S, EGG BUCKLAND

Grid Reference: SX498578.   Public access (in overgrown corner of churchyard).

St Edmund's Well.

Egg Buckland (the word Buckland probably means that the boundaries of the manor here were described in an Anglo-Saxon Charter hence 'Bookland') has a church which has been dedicated to Edward the Martyr since 1161; Edward was the grandson of the Saxon Earl of Devon and was assassinated, when he was only sixteen years old, by nobles who favoured his half brother. After his death, miracles are said to have occurred at his grave in Wareham Priory. The Holy Well at Egg Buckland was used by the church for baptisms but this has not been so for many years. Today the spring is hidden by debris and undergrowth in the top corner of the churchyard where a trickle of water issues from the ground to find its way between the gravestones.

Traditional Uses: Baptisms.

Other places in Greater Plymouth where there are traditions of a Holy Well, or references to wells of ancient lineage:
St Andrew's Well – near the Lairy, associated with an ancient fig tree, has healing properties.
St Catherine's Well – located in Ham Grounds.
Buckwell – near the Barbican.
Finewell – somewhere near Prysten House.
St John's Well – in Benson Meadows, Houndiscombe, curative for skin complaints.
Jacob's Well – Southside Street.
Maudlyn Well – North Hill near site of the leper hospital.
Ladywell – place name evidence near Pennycross.
Plympton St Maurice – St Thomas's well – near Pathfields, shown on Saltram estate map.

Parish: Ringmore
Ordnance Survey Explorer Map OL20

At the time of the Domesday Book in 1086, Ringmore was a manor held from the king by Judhael of Totnes and was worth 30 shillings in taxable value; in addition to 6 villagers and 6 smallholders there were 2 slaves here. Judel or Iudhael, as he is also known, was one of six landowners in Devon who between them held three-quarters of all the Devon manors recorded in Domesday. One of the smallholdings in the manor was Marewilde (Marwell).

39 ST MARY'S WELL, MARWELL
Grid Reference: SX653472. Good public access; the well is by the roadside.

Just below Marwell Crossroads on the left-hand side of the road, stands a pretty little stone built well-house of probable early 19th century date. A carved cross on the apex of the gable end marks this as a holy place. It is a very charming spot where the cool water from the spring is refreshing on a hot summer's day.

The name of the well is possibly a Christian dedication but more likely arose from an early interpretation of the personal name of one of the smallholders.

Traditional Uses: Lost.

St Mary's Well, Marwell.

Parish: Bigbury
Ordnance Survey Explorer Map OL20

No visit to the South Hams would be truly complete without a visit to Burgh Island which lies a few hundred yards offshore and separated from it at low tide by a strand of golden sand, and at other times by a shallow but fast-flowing current. Visits here at early morning or out of the holiday season are the best times to appreciate the magic of this little island. The landscape of the parish is one of rolling fertile countryside dotted with small settlements.

40. ST ANNE'S WELL, ST ANNE'S CHAPEL
Grid Reference: SX664474.

The area where this well is to be found was included in an Anglo-Saxon Charter of AD846 which describes the general area, but the chapel of St Anne is not mentioned until 1242. The site of the Holy Well is along the lane from Holywell Stores which leads to Holliwell Farm and where a spring of water feeds into a slate trough on the left

St Anne's Well.

of the pathway. At some time during the 1960s, the original well site was covered over by the landowner as he is reported to have got 'fed up' with people visiting it. However, the spring still flows from this place which was in the field a few yards up the hill.

What remains of the chapel of St Anne is now built into one of the internal walls of the pub on the crossroads.

Traditional Uses: Lost.

41 ST MILBURGA'S WELL, AVETON GIFFORD
Grid Reference: SX683468. Good public access; a tidal ford over the road.

This site is a fascinating example of how local Devonshire traditions were influenced by legends from elsewhere. St Milburga was the abbess of the monastery at Much Wenlock in Shropshire which had been founded by her father, Theodore the second Archbishop of Canterbury (he is credited with creating the structure of the Anglo-Saxon Church). A local prince in Shropshire tried to compel Milburga to marry him but she refused him and fled across a river. Armed men were sent after her and, to prevent capture, she prayed for divine help at which the river rose and blocked her pursuers. Milburga escaped and went on to become a much respected leader of her monastery where she died in AD737.

Tidal ford to St Milburga's Well.

Close to the tidal ford over the river near Aveton Gifford, an ancient chapel and Holy Well were dedicated to St Milburga, a dedication inspired by the story of rising waters which protected a virgin's honour and enabled her to go on and do good works. The well was lost when garden landscaping works were carried out late last century; but in the private garden next to the public footpath there is a most interesting looking old building which seems to feed water into an ornamental pond. This may not be the site of the Holy Well and chapel, nevertheless, the footpath provides a most enjoyable walk circular along the river and through the woods, and the chance to think about St Milburga and her trust in the power of her faith.

Traditional Uses: Lost.

Parish: Loddiswell
Ordnance Survey Explorer Map OL20

A pretty village with some excellent walks in nearby Woodland Trust woodlands. The River Avon forms the eastern boundary to the parish and was once an important fishery, paying thirty salmon each year as tribute to Judhael of Totnes.

42 LODD'S WELL
Grid Reference: SX722486. Good public access; well is alongside a village pathway.

This is a site which is still valued by local people who restored it as a Local Heritage Project as part of the village Millennium celebrations. Wildflowers and herbs have been planted around the cobbled yard which is provided with pavings for sitting and collecting water from the spring. The water was tested for purity and is now collected by some people in the village and used as an alternative to supermarket bottled water.

A few yards away from Lodd's Well an old butterwell by the roadside has also been restored; this interest confirms the value which people here still place on the naming of their parish. Well done Loddiswell!

Traditional Uses: Water supply but other traditions lost.

Above: *Butterwell, Loddiswell.*
Left: *Lodd's Well.*

Parish: Halwell
Ordnance Survey Explorer Map OL20

The earliest records name the settlement here after a Holy Well – in Domesday Book it is called Hagewile and it is one of only two places in Devon which has carried this name since recorded history (the other is Halwill, Well 21). There is an Iron Age fort in the parish and the strategic importance of Halwell was confirmed when it became one of only four places in Devon designated by the Anglo-Saxons as 'burghs' meaning strongholds (the others were Exeter, Pilton and Lydford). Halwell later lost its role when the castle at Totnes was built after the Norman Conquest. The continuity of the place name suggests that the Holy Well here is of very early origin, possibly dating to the Celtic period, and before the introduction of Christianity to Devon.

43 HOLY WELL

Grid Reference: SX777532. Good public access; the spring is in the churchyard.

Right: *Preaching Cross, St Leonard's churchyard.*
Far right: *Site of Holy Well.*

The tithe map of 1840 shows the 'holy spring' close to the church of St Leonard. Today there is little to mark the spot apart from a gully and some stonework near the east wall of the church which probably shows where the spring was to be found. The water seems to have been channelled away and it is a disappointment to find that this most ancient of sacred water places is no longer marked and celebrated.

Traditional Uses: Lost.

Parish: Totnes
Ordnance Survey Explorer Map OL20

Since Norman times, when it became the base for Judhael and the extensive lands he held from the king, Totnes has been an important centre for the South

Hams. An impressive castle was built here and its ruins still dominate part of the town. As a port and trading centre, the town prospered in the 15th and 16th centuries and many fine buildings remain from that time. Today it is a place with a special character and energy. Dartington Hall and the Schumacher College just outside the town are renowned centres for the arts and literature and, with the Cider Press Crafts Centre, they make Totnes an enjoyable place to see as part of any visit to the Holy Wells of the South Hams.

44 LEECHWELL

Grid Reference: SX801603. Good public access down Leechwell Lane which is an ancient, narrow but fairly easy pathway next to the Kingsbridge Inn.

No pilgrimage to Devon's Holy Wells can be complete until you have seen Leechwell. A large stone-walled enclosure protects three water spouts which flow into separate stone troughs. The enclosure is often festooned with flowers, ribbons and offerings from those who still come here to experience the spirit of this place.

Leechwell.

The water spouts have names: Long Crippler which is a cure for problems of the eyes, Toad is a cure for skin problems, and Snake for snake bites and disorders of the spirit. The well was used as a source of water for the town and may have been connected with a leper hospital which existed near here in the Middle Ages. One of the most ancient and important Holy Wells in Devon.

Traditional Uses: Healing and fortune telling.

45. HARPER'S WELL
Grid Reference: SX798603. Good public access, and although the lane is steep, the spring water runs into a trough where the lane meets the road.

Harper's Well.

A lane from the town leads up to Harper's Hill and on to West Down, and along this lane a number of springs feed into a channel which runs into a stone trough at a point where the lane meets the A381 road. From here the water is channelled below ground to the moat of the castle which it has been feeding since at least the 15th century. Towards the top of the lane the land is known locally as 'fairwells' and a deep well was found there some years ago; this has now been lost again but was reported to be shaped 'like an inverted light bulb' and lined with stone.

Traditional Uses: Healing.

Other Parishes:
Other places in South Hams where there are traditions of a Holy Well or references to wells of ancient lineage include:

Ashprington – healing well recorded in 1605.
Brixton – place name Haliwill in a document of 1242.
Dartington – dripping well cures for eyes.
Dartmouth – wishing well in a document of 1451 also a Holy Well near a chapel dedicated to St Michael.
Dittisham – Holy Well near Halwell Farm and chapel to St Michael in a document of 1452.
South Milton – Holywille mentioned in a document of 1447.
Stoke Gabriel – Holy Well near Howill Cottage.
Marlborough – Holy Well.
West Alvington – Sockwell; cures for eyes.

TEIGNBRIDGE AND TORBAY DISTRICT

Parish: Ashburton
Ordnance Survey Explorer Map OL28

In 1086 the Manor of Ashburton (Essebretone) was held by the Bishop of Exeter. The entry in the Domesday Book includes 10 slaves here. Domesday lists 3233 slaves in Devon, a higher proportion than anywhere else in the South West with the exception of Cornwall, which suggests that they were members of the native Celtic population who had lost their freedom. Ashburton became a borough in 1238 and was one of the five Stannary towns which controlled every aspect of the exploitation of the tin mines of Dartmoor and beyond. Ashburton today is a thriving centre with a little town museum and some splendid antique and secondhand bookshops to explore before visiting the four Holy Well sites here, and then setting out along the network of footpaths and roadways which lead out on to the moor and the surrounding countryside.

46 ST GUDULA'S WELL
Grid Reference: SX754694. Good public access; site is by the roadside although there is a flight of shallow steps down to the actual well.

St Gudula's Well.

This is one of the best-cared-for sites in Devon. An ancient stone cross stands by the roadside on the Old Totnes Road and from here a flight of steps leads down to the well. A plaque on the wall confirms that the well is named after St Gudula but who was this saint? Some traditions say that the name is a local interpretation of St Gulwell who is also known as St Wulvella, and was the sister of Saint Sidwell of Exeter. Others say that it is indeed the Saint Gudula who died in AD712 and became the patron of Brussels' Cathederal. The plaque was erected in 1933 when Saint Gudula's name was favoured, but since then scholarly opinion has supported St Wulvella as the patron of the well (she is also remembered at Gulval in Cornwall).

The cross was returned to its original site in 1933 at which time the well was also restored. Since then some local roadworks have reduced the flow of water from the spring into the stone trough at the well-head but some minor clearing of debris should remedy this.

Traditional Uses: Cure for eye problems.

St Gudula's cross.

47 LADYWELL

Grid Reference: SX758698. Good public access; well site can be reached on foot along surfaced paths.

Old records show a well in Ladywell Orchard close to the ancient chapel of St Lawrence; the orchard has long gone. Today the clue is a tiny group of houses called Ladywell Square and from where an alleyway leads along the bottom of some gardens which are the remains of the orchard; here the boundary wall curves to accommodate a large granite trough (now filled with soil and plants). This trough once received water from the spring which was Ladywell and in the 18th and 19th centuries it was used as a domestic water supply for the surrounding cottages; an open channel of drainage tiles shows where the overflow went along the alley into the town drainage system.

Ladywell.

Traditional Uses: Lost.

Dropping Well.

48 DROPPING WELL

Grid Reference: SX751693. Good public access; the well is in a bank on the roadside.

This is a stone trough set into a boundary bank alongside the Western Road and close to Peartree Cross which is the old junction of the roads from Totnes, Buckfastleigh and the road across the moor. It is spring fed from above and its location suggests that it was a convenient watering place for those journeying through Ashburton.

Traditional Uses: Lost.

49 STIDWELL

Grid Reference: SX735729. Good public access but uphill across some uneven moorland.

Stidwell.

This is an interesting site as the parish boundary between Ashburton and Buckland-in-the-Moor is deliberately shaped to fit around the site of the spring. A document of c.1200 calls this place Blindwell. As late as 1771 a boundary dispute was settled by providing a drinking trough at Stidwell which was half in one parish and half in the other so that there was equal access to the water from the spring.

The substantial granite block wall which forms the boundary here runs from the road to Buckland up on to the moor towards Buckland Beacon, and Stidwell is to be found where this curves and another wall joins it to form a small enclosure. A jumble of stones marks the site of the spring although the drinking trough has gone.

Traditional Uses: Lost.

Parish: Widecombe-in-the-Moor
Ordnance Survey Explorer Map OL28

This area is so much a part of the tourist trail that further introduction is not necessary. However it is a special place and those walking through it on the eastern route of the Two Moors Way, and visitors who come by road, should take time to look at the field patterns in the vale and note that in the parish there is a Venton Bridge and a Venton Farm (venton being the Celtic word for well).

50 SAXON WELL
Grid Reference: SX718768. Good public access; the well is by the road-side just below the Post Office in the centre of the village.

One of the prettiest wells in Devon although its antiquity is difficult to establish. Perhaps this is the well from which, according to a local legend, the people of Widecombe gave the devil a drink when he rode into the village on 21 October 1638; as he swallowed the water it sizzled as it went down his throat! The villagers then saw him hitch his horse to the church steeple which fell with a crash (another version

Saxon Well.

is that the church was hit by lightning and four people were killed). The well-house is certainly of the right date for the legend and the spring is said never to run dry. It has gathered a reputation as a wishing well but older traditions speak of its healing powers.

Traditional Uses: Cure for problems of the eye.

Parish: Bovey Tracey
Ordnance Survey Explorer Map 110

A favourite little town with much to see and do. The headquarters of the Dartmoor National Park Authority is here and so too is the splendid Devon Guild of Craftsmen which has a display of the work of the very best craftsmen and women from the county (and an excellent café).

51 ST MARY'S WELL
Grid Reference: SX821786. Good public access; the well is by the roadside next to the parish church.

St Mary's Well.

This is an impressive site with a massive granite trough set under an arched well-house standing close to the ancient church of Peter and Paul. The water from this well is associated with the story of the Virgin Mary and the golden frogs. There are two versions of the story; one describes how the Holy Mother was seen coming down Trough Lane; she drank from the spring which feeds the well and ever after the water was used for baptisms. The second story tells how long ago a poor but devout sexton of the church returned from the well with two pitchers of water and found an unknown visitor at his gate; he welcomed this stranger in.

The visitor blessed the water and the family and promised them long life and grandchildren to care for their old age; after this she left and went to pray at the well and said 'Here you have living water for the church and yourselves forever.' From that day the frogs which live around the well are golden in colour in remembrance of her visit.

Today the trough is often dry and the spring does not provide a home for golden frogs; perhaps if the flow of water could be restored they would return. Make what you will of old legends such as this one; what wonderful stories they are. This is a site which deserves to be a local treasure.

Traditional Uses: Baptisms and healing.

Parishes: Newton Abbot and Kingsteignton
Ordnance Survey Explorer Map 110

Newton Abbot was once a major railway town and remains an important market centre. It has a long and proud history and a number of hidden gems such as Ford House (now part of the local authority's offices) and Bradley Manor (a National Trust property) which deserve much wider appreciation. The village of Kingsteignton is now almost a suburb of its neighbour but at the time of the Domesday Book in 1086 it was held by the king (Teintone) as the chief manor of Teignton Hundred.

52 ST MARY'S WELL
Grid Reference: SX856715. Good public access; the well is adjacent to the pavement by the site of St Mary's Church (now turned into living accommodation) near the cattle market.

A metal grill by the pavement and a small plaque underneath the former church marks this spring which once supplied water and healing to travellers on the old main road from Exeter to Dartmouth. In 1993 the church was converted into flats and the opportunity was taken to refurbish the ancient spring. St Mary's Church existed from the 14th century and was once the principal place of worship. Its congregation declined and this grew worse in the 19th century when a church was built a short distance away in the new residential district of Abbotsbury. In 1849 a report for the General Board of Health

St Mary's Well.

found that parts of Newton Abbot had a death rate in excess of 25 per cent due to damp housing conditions and a poor water supply; at that time the well at St Mary's was still used but seems to have been discontinued when the Board's recommendation for 'a constant water supply be laid on in every street' was implemented.

Traditional Uses: Lost.

53 HONEYWELL, KINGSTEIGNTON
Grid Reference: SX871729. Good public access; the well is behind the churchyard at Kingsteignton along a little path with a few steps in the east corner.

Honeywell, Kingsteignton.

A small enclosure at the side of a garden where there is a flow of clear water running into a trough which is approached down a few shallow steps; the bottom step is an old stone slab with some lettering which it is now difficult to decipher. Water from the well has been collected for its healing properties and was used to good effect within living memory on the sprained ankle of a local footballer.

Traditional Uses: General curative properties.

54 FAIRWATER, KINGSTEIGNTON
Grid Reference: SX870728. Good public access; this is a stream of water which runs through the churchyard.

A spring rises in the hills some way from the church and the water was channelled through the village and churchyard at some time during the 12th or 13th century to provide power to a number of mills which operated here. A local legend tells how the stream dried up but was restored to full flow when a ram was sacrificed. Ever since, Kingsteignton has celebrated with a Ram Roasting Fair.

Traditional Uses: Lost.

Parish: Bishopsteignton
Ordnance Survey Explorer Map 110

Overlooking the estuary of the River Teign, land in this parish was owned by the bishops of Exeter from the earliest times. A country residence for Bishop Grandisson was built here in the 14th century but within 200 years, this grand house and chapel was already in ruins. Some walls of the palace still remain standing and give an impression of what it must have been like during its heyday.

Above: *Fairwater Well.*
Left: *Bishop's Palace.*

55 WHITEWELL

Grid Reference: SX913749. Good public access from a car park on Teignmouth golfcourse but the footpath down to the well is uneven and steep.

This well is sited on the hill some way above the site of the old Bishop's Palace and is approached down a track through heathland and trees. It is a curious circular structure some 2 metres deep and sunk into the limestone rock. There is a ruin of a 19th century pump house nearby but water from the well now seeps away into the woodland and hillside undergrowth. This spot does not have a happy atmosphere.

Traditional Uses: Curative especially for fevers also fortune telling.

Whitewell.

Parish: Dawlish
Ordnance Survey Explorer Map 110

Dawlish town is a well-known seaside resort and inland from the coast there is interesting rolling countryside with heath and woodland to explore.

56 LIDWELL

Grid Reference: SX924761. Good public access but only by footpath across some uneven and steep land with at least one stile to climb.

The note of an unhappy atmosphere given to the nearby Whitewell (Well 55) should also be applied to this site and with good reason. Tucked under the hill are the remains of a small 13th century chantry chapel which was dedicated to the Virgin Mary and was occupied by a monk or clergyman who gained a reputation for luring travellers to the chapel and then robbing and killing them. After the Reformation in the 16th century, the chapel was abandoned and when the well was investigated it was found to contain the bones of several women and children.

Today it is a lonely spot and the water of the well is black and devoid of life.

Traditional Uses: Lost.

Lidwell.

Parishes: The 'Well' parishes of Coffinswell, Abbottskerswell, Kingskerswell, West and East Ogwell
Ordnance Survey Explorer Map 110

Lying close to Newton Abbot, these five parishes were attached to their well names by the time the Domesday Book was compiled in 1086. This is limestone country where surface water can quickly sink underground and so the presence of unfailing natural springs may have been of special importance.

The two Ogwell parishes took their name from a Saxon landowner called Wocca or Wogga (they were called wogganwille in a Charter of AD956). The two Kerswells are named after the 'cresswells' one of which was held by the church and one by the king. Coffinswell is named for a family who owned land here and elsewhere in Devon. With such ancient lineage, it is disappointing that the remaining evidence for the ancient wells in the five parishes is rather sparse.

57 EAST AND WEST OGWELL
Grid Reference: SX839701. Good public access to both churches.

East Ogwell.

St Bartholomew's Church lies in the centre of the village of East Ogwell. Next to it there is a field where a stone drain brings spring water to a marshy area where wild watercress grows in summer. This may be the spring which fed the original well but there is no local information about it now readily available.

West Ogwell has more to offer the pilgrim. The church here stands apart on a low hill; and it is rare in Devon for having escaped any major internal restoration work. Apart from the Georgian box pews, its interior is almost as it would have been in the Middle Ages and an atmosphere of quiet spirituality still pervades the building which is now under the care of the Churches Conservation Trust.

In 1892 an ancient well called Hobbin's or Holbeam well and 'similar in design to Fice's well in Dartmoor' (Well 28) was noted here 'close to the site of a manor which formerly existed here but of which no trace now remains.' There is a settlement called Holbeam across the valley from West Ogwell church and it may be that the old well seen in 1892 existed somewhere close by.

West Ogwell Church.

58 LADYWELL, ABBOTSKERSWELL
Grid Reference: SX858685. Good public access along public footpath from Butcher's Arms.

Ladywell, Abbotskerswell.

At the time of the Domesday Book, the manor of Abbotskerswell was held by Horton Abbey in Dorset. Anglo-Saxon documents called this place 'cresswell' and it appears that from early times the spring supplied a plentiful crop of wild or perhaps cultivated, watercress. The parish church has been dedicated to St Mary since the 18th century and the naming of the well suggests that she was also the medieval patron. The wellhouse has been restored and fitted with a new door which protects a stone-lined basin filled with clear water from the spring.

Traditional Uses: Lost.

Kingskerswell has a similar history to Abbotskerswell and the church is also dedicated to Mary. Clear streams of water flow past the church but the area has been much changed by road and railway building and the site of the 'kerswell' is uncertain.

59 COFFINSWELL

Grid Reference: SX891688. Good public access; the well is by the roadside.

Coffinswell.

An attractive little village where the tiny brick well-house is tucked in by the roadside in front of a thatched cottage called Old Well Cottage. The well-house is of 19th–20th century origins and it seems likely that the original spring (welle in Domesday Book) is somewhere in the adjacent garden. There is a legend that a young woman was refused burial in the churchyard of St Bartholomew and that each New Year after the stroke of midnight, she takes a 'cock's stride' towards the churchyard which is a little way up the hill. The church here is kept locked.

Traditional Uses: Fortune telling.

Parish: Torbay
Ordnance Survey Explorer Map 110

Torbay is one of Devon's premier resorts but it had a long history before it became a fashionable seaside town. At the time of the Domesday Book in 1086, the manor was known as Torre and was held by one of the king's servants, William the Usher. In 1196 a new abbey was founded here as a house of Premonstratensian monks whose Order had been established in Paris in 1121 and who already had a number of monasteries in England. At that time, the main church in Torre was dedicated to St Petroc and the story of how the nearby Holy Well became St Elfride's Well, is an interesting example of how history can become confused over time and through misreading of evidence.

60 ST ELFRIDE'S WELL, TORRE
Grid Reference: SX909645. Good public access; the well is set into a wall beside the pavement opposite the old parish church of Torre.

St Elfride's Well, Torre.

Despite its rather unremarkable appearance this well has a remarkable story to tell. The church is now the Greek Orthodox Church of St Andrew but was once the parish church of St Saviour's (and before that it was dedicated to St Petroc). At the time when nearby Torre Abbey was founded, St Petroc's was the parish church for Torre (or Tormohun) and near the church was a Holy Well. In addition there seems to have been two small chapels in the parish, one dedicated to St Michael and one to St Saviour, close to where the new abbey was to be built. The Charter which granted land for the abbey, mentioned the boundary as being the 'efrideswell – the everflowing stream'; some 34 years later the canons of the abbey were also granted 'all the water which comes from the spring of St Petroc.'

At some point St Petroc's Holy Well and Elfride's Well became confused. This was compounded in 1860 when the then vicar of the parish church rebuilt the Holy Well opposite the parish church (which by then was called St Saviour's). Knowing that there was a Saxon Saint called Elfreda of Glastonbury, he seems to have decided that she must be the true patron of the well and it became St Elfrida's. When the area around it was developed, the local authority then called it St Elfrida's Road; which it is today! In recent years the well has been known as 'Freddy's Well' by local people.

So this walled-up Victorian well has a long and confused history but one which can be traced back to that foremost of Celtic Saints, St Petroc of Bodmin.

Traditional Uses: Curative powers especially for skin complaints.

Other Parishes:

Some other places in Teignbridge where there are traditions of a Holy Well or references to wells of ancient lineage:

Bovey Tracey – Ashwell at Whitstone. Associated with a Palm Sunday rite and curative for skin conditions.

Chagford – St John's Well. Located near the church but now filled in. Pixy Well, near Fernworthy, a wishing well in which a pin was floated to make a wish.

Chudleigh – Several wells associated with the Bishop's Palace also a Holy Water Well in Ugbrooke Park 'Kerswell' or Nanny Pedric's Well in Kerswell Orchard and Wapper Well marked on 1819 Tithe Map.

Combeinteignhead – Wishing well near the church associated with a famous old cork tree. Holy Well Cottage near Combe Cellars.

Denbury – Halwell Farm place name.

Hennock – Ladywell; a well existed in a field some distance from Teign Village but has been obliterated by a reservoir.

Ideford – Place name evidence.

Kenn – Dripwell a spring located in grounds of Trelill; curative for eyes.

Manaton – Place name evidence.

Moretonhampstead – Several wells including St Anne's Well, Job's Well and Jacob's Well.

Newton Abbot – Bradley Spring, near Bradley Manor and curative for eyes.

Torquay – Holy Well near Torwood Street (may be shown in a painting in the museum).

EXETER AND EAST DEVON DISTRICT

Parish: City of Exeter
Ordnance Survey Explorer Map 114

Following the departure of the Second Legion of the Roman army in AD75, a new civil administration centre was built at Isca Dumnoniorum (Exeter) and this was occupied until the 5th century when large parts seemed to have been abandoned. The reason why so many people left Isca may have been related to the changes which were taking place following the end of Roman rule in Britain, and the pressures from the east caused by waves of invading Anglo-Saxons. Although the central parts of the settlement fell into decay, it is certain that people from the Celtic tribes continued to live in the areas around and about. The legend of one of Devon's most famous daughters, Saint Sativola (or St Sidwell as she is mostly known), and the Holy Well which was named after her comes from this period of history.

St Sidwell was one of the children of a local family (one of her sisters became St Wulvella) and she seemed to have been an especially virtuous maid who had been converted to the Christian faith. Her virtue was her undoing as her jealous stepmother incited some local labourers to attack the girl with their haymaking scythes. They beheaded the young maiden and from the spot where her head fell, a spring of pure water sprang up from the ground. Some four days later the ghost of Saint Sidwell was seen carrying her severed head and, following this vision, a church in her honour and to house her body was built

Icon of St Sidwell.

nearby. Miracles of healing the sick and the lame followed and a significant cult of St Sidwell of Exeter developed during the next centuries; windows in Exeter Cathedral and in All Souls College Oxford were dedicated to her and altars to the memory of St Sidwell were placed in churches in Cornwall, Devon and Somerset.

In the 12th century, water from St Sidwell's Holy Well was piped to the Cathedral Close and to St Nicholas' Priory. In 1349 a new aqueduct was commissioned by the cathedral authorities; this still used water from the well (via a well-house at Well Head) and part of the water supply system which developed from this was laid in the tunnels which are known today as the Underground Passages.

In AD880 the central part of Exeter was re-founded by the Anglo-Saxons as one of their four defended towns in Devon; from that time St Sidwell has been remembered as a Saxon and not a Celtic Saint. The year of her martyrdom is uncertain and so it is now impossible to say whether she was a Celtic or Saxon maid. What is certain is that St Sidwell of Exeter and the Holy Well associated with her, are important parts of Devon's heritage.

61 ST SIDWELL'S HOLY WELL
Grid Reference: SX925932. Public access to the roads in the general area.

The parish of St Sidwell is outside the original city boundaries but in the 18th and 19th centuries it became one of the most populous in Exeter, with cottages and new streets being built, rebuilt and altered. During this process the actual site of the Holy Well has become lost. In 1857 a well was disturbed when the London & South Western Railway was cut through this area, and this may have been the lost St Sidwell's Holy Well or could have been Cathedral Well (Well 62). As late as 1870 St Sidwell's Holy Well was believed to be near the junction of York Road and Oxford Street. There is a Well Street here, and some Sidwella Cottages, but no evidence of the beehive shaped well–house which is shown in the Cathedral's Saint Sidwell window. We are left only with the interesting fibreglass sculpture on the frontage in Sidwell Street and some place names but nothing as a fitting memorial to Exeter's saint in the place where she was martyred.

Traditional Uses: Curative for skin and eye diseases.

62 CATHEDRAL WELL (ALSO KNOWN AS ST SIDWELL'S)
Grid Reference: SX926936. Good public access but down some steps at St James's Halt Station.

Above: Relief mural of St Sidwell above shop-front.
Above left: Sidwella Cottages, Well Street.

When the railway came through the area, a well supplying the cathedral community was disturbed; the water supply was diverted and the well building was moved to the side of the steps down to St James's Station. Today a bricked up little well-house can still be found amongst the tangle of growth near the platform. It has not been possible to establish whether this is also the original St Sidwell's Holy Well or a later well-head used to pipe the water across the city. In the absence of a better candidate, perhaps this well should be renovated in memory of St Sidwell.

Traditional Uses: Lost.

Cathedral Well.

63 PARKER'S WELL
Grid Reference: SX927918. Good public access; the well is by the road-side near the junction of Topsham Road and Matford Lane.

Although the water has now been diverted into the road drains, this is a pretty little arched well. It gave its name to Parker's Well House which was destroyed during the air raids of the Second World War but fortunately the original stones of the well remained.

Traditional Uses: Curative for eye diseases.

Parker's Well.

There are records of a number of other ancient and Holy Wells in Exeter but they are now difficult or impossible to find:

St Anne's Well: (also sometimes called St Agnes's Well) this was located in the same general area as St Sidwell's Holy Well and close to the chapel of St Anne which stands, as it has done for more than 600 years, at the top of Sidwell Street. Water from this well was piped across the city to a brewery near the Iron Bridge and known as St Anne's Brewery.

St Martin's Well: located at the edge of Cathedral Close; this was claimed to be a Roman well (possibly located in the cellars of the Royal Clarence Hotel).
St Mary's Well: associated with the Saxon Minster.
Bride's Well: mentioned in a Charter of AD938 and possibly on boundary between old parishes of Stoke Canon and Wonford.
Gubb's Well: in St Thomas area; documentary evidence in 1797.

Parish: Broadclyst
Ordnance Survey Explorer Map 114

This village is linked to nearby Killerton House which was the home of the Acland family from the time of James I when it was purchased for the widow of Sir John Acland who had been knighted by the king. Killerton was remodelled in the 18th century and over the following 100 years, the grounds of the estate benefited from exotic plants sent back from all over the world, including the first seeds in England of the Californian Redwood tree. Today the house and grounds and much of the village are in the care of the National Trust and there are many pleasant walks around the estate.

64 HOLY WELL
Grid Reference: SS991009. Good public access; in roadside copse owned by the National Trust (but the short pathway can be overgrown).

Some people say that this is the prettiest Holy Well in Devon. It is built of local stone in the Romanesque style and probably dates from the time in the late 19th century when improvements were being made to the estate at Killerton by Sir Thomas Acland; water from the well is still piped away for use on the estate.

Two steps lead down to the water which is pure and clear. The spring is certainly of ancient origin and is located close to a settlement and farm called Beare – Old English sacred grove.

Holy Well.

Traditional Uses: Lost.

Parish: Dunkeswell
Ordnance Survey Explorer Map 115

Dunkeswell is a Saxon village which took its name from the Saxon owner of the water source in the centre of the settlement which is set in the lee of the Blackdown Hills. This is an Area of Outstanding Natural Beauty which stretches across the border between Somerset and Devon and has a distinctive landscape, rich in wildlife and historical interest. The villages and hamlets of the Blackdowns are worthy of discovery and exploration. The parish church at Dunkeswell was dedicated on 5 December 1259 by Bishop Bronescombe of Exeter and ever since there has been confusion about the name of the patron saint. It has been variously recorded as 'unknown', Nicholas, and Patrick. It is believed that the original dedication was to Petroc which was sometimes spelt as Patrick by clerks of earlier times. Today the dedication is to St Nicholas.

In 1201 twelve Cistercian monks from Forde Abbey near Chard, travelled to Dunkeswell to start work on building an abbey on land which had been granted to them by Lord William Brewer, the High Sheriff of Devon (he had also given land at Torre in South Devon to the Premonstratensian Order for an abbey there). The site was some two miles from the parish church, and was supplied with pure water from two steams and the River Madford. Dunkeswell Abbey flourished and at one time held lands as far away as Buckland Brewer in North Devon, but it was not without problems; the Black Death in 1348 killed many of the monks and in 1508 there were allegations of riotous behaviour. Thirty years later John Tregonwell, commissioner for the king, rode up to the abbey with an order for its dissolution and the 380 years of history of this place was ended. John Russell, who was given the abbey by the Crown, quickly sold off the buildings for demolition. Today the ruins of the abbey can still be seen and something of the peace and sense of spirit still remains here by the quietly running brook.

65 ST PETROC'S WELL
Grid Reference: ST141077. Good public access; the site is by the roadside some 100 yards south of the parish church.

What was once a well of clear water is now hidden under an ornamental village seating area. Until recent times the village pump which took water

St Petroc's Well.

from the well, was a centre where people from the village met to exchange information and gossip, but today it no longer seems to serve that function.

Traditional Uses: Lost.

Parish: Woodbury
Ordnance Survey Explorer Map 115

This is an area of extensive heathland and woods which flourish on the East Devon Pebblebeds which were formed during the Triassic Period some 150 million years ago. In places the commons are used by the military, but there is good walking to be had and the East Devon Way is just one of the many tracks which provide varied rambles and a chance to explore Devon's largest natural landscape outside the National Parks.

Goldenwell.

66 GOLDENWELL

Grid Reference: SY032848. Good public access; the site is in woodland, close to a public footpath only a few yards from the road.

This well is on Lympstone Common and is situated near a boundary stone which marks the boundary between East Budleigh and Withycombe Raleigh (Hayes Barton once the home of Sir Walter Raleigh, is only a mile away). Today it is a marshy hollow with a small pool of black water to mark the spot, and why it is called Goldenwell is difficult to say; possibly it was a place where offerings were thrown into the spring, or perhaps it gained its name from the golden heath grasses which grow on the Common.

Traditional Uses: Lost.

67 WOODBURY SALTERTON WELL

Grid Reference: SY013890. Good public access; the well is by the road-side in the village.

Woodbury Salterton Well.

This is a good example of a water supply (and some good Biblical advice) provided by a local worthy for the benefit of the villagers. The attractive well-house has some interesting stone carving and an inscription from the Book of Revelations over the entrance:

And let him that thirst come.
And whosever will,
Let him take the water of life freely.

A flight of steps leads down to a curved iron pipe which was the water source. This well is a pleasant feature, probably of Victorian origin, but does not seem to be highly valued by local people today.

Traditional Uses: Lost.

Other Parishes:

Some other places in East Devon where there are traditions of a Holy Well or references to wells of ancient lineage:

Awliscombe – traditions of a Holy Well for cures of problems of the eye.

Bradninch – old Baptising Well associated with Trinity Chapel.

Colyton – place name evidence at Whitwell.

Honiton – Holyshute a spring at Holyshute House and possibly of 16th century origin.

Seaton – a number of ancient wells here including Eyewell and site of a possible Roman well which was excavated in early 20th century.

Tiverton – Hobby Horse Well in St Andrew's Street.

Woodbury – Soldier's Well and Jacob's Well on Commons.

MID DEVON DISTRICT

Parish: Crediton
Ordnance Survey Explorer Map 114

Crediton has a special place in the history of the spread of Christianity in Europe through the works of St Boniface who was born here some time around AD675. This was the period when the Anglo-Saxons had defeated the Celtic Dumnonii in the east of their territory and were moving westwards. Boniface, or Wynfrith as he was first known, had a mother who was the daughter of a local Celtic chief and a father who was an important Anglo-Saxon. Boniface was called to the religious life and studied at the Anglo-Saxon Minster at Exeter and then at an abbey near Winchester. Because of his home background, Boniface would have been aware of the Celtic Church and its differences from the Roman tradition; in his own ministry he became a fervent advocate of Rome, to the extent that he actively supported the suppression of Celtic teaching. Before starting his work to convert the peoples of Germany in AD722, Boniface took an oath to the Pope which makes clear his total adherence to the Roman Church:
I will in no way oppose the unity of the one universal Church, no matter who may seek to persuade me. And if comes to my knowledge that priests have turned from the ancient practices of the holy fathers, I will have no intercourse or connection with them but rather, if I can, will restrain them. If I cannot, I will at once faithfully make known the whole matter to my apostolic lord.

So the great Christian son of Crediton was no lover of the Celtic tradition. He would also have known of the ancient pagan beliefs in nature spirits as the area near where he was born was the centre of the complex of sacred groves, which the Roman fort at North Tawton had been established to control. The Nymet and Beara names which tell us of these ancient holy places, occur today in Nymet Rowland, Nymet Tracey, Nichols Nymet, George Nympton, King's Nympton, Broadsnymet, Beare Farm, Great Beer etc. When Boniface felled Thor's Oak at Geismar to show the pagan German tribes the error of their beliefs, perhaps he was also striking a blow against the customs of his ancient

Devon ancestors. While the tradition he represented was successful, the old memories and observances lived on under the guise of the Green Man (whose image appears in Exeter Cathedral and at least 18 parish churches), and at some of the Holy Wells of Devon.

68 ST WYNEFRED'S WELL

Grid Reference: SS835003. Good public access; the well is in a public park and sports field.

The stone well-house has been much renovated and stands today close to a statue of Boniface who may have mixed feelings about a Holy Well named after him! Nevertheless it is good to find a carefully tended link with the earliest history of the town.

Traditional Uses: Curative for problems of the eye.

69 LIBBETT'S WELL

Grid Reference: SS834002. Good public access; the well is down a narrow path near the magnificent parish church.

This is a striking site with an arch over a stone channel which contains running water. It is close to the church and also the site of an ancient priest's hostel, and possibly a leper hospital. Recently the tradition of leaving gifts of flowers and other offerings has been re-introduced to this well.

Traditional Uses: Curative for problems of the eye and general healing properties.

Above: *St Wynefred's Well.*
Left: *Libbett's Well.*

Ladywell.

70 LADYWELL

Grid Reference: SX825987. Public access but down a rough and overgrown track by the side of an old cob farm wall.

At the time of the Domesday Book in 1086, the Bishop of Exeter held the Manor of Crediton, and one of the holdings which made up the estate was Youweton or Uton. The dedication of the well here suggests a medieval date and in the 12th century there was a chantry chapel at Uton. Today the site it is neglected and the spring is hard to find amongst the undergrowth, dumped agricultural rubbish and drainage pipes which litter the area around. Rather a sad place.

Traditional Uses: Curative for problems of the eye.

Parish: Cullompton
Ordnance Survey Explorer Map 115

Today it is easy to speed past Cullompton on the M5, but if you travel to the town along the old roads you will pass through deep countryside of rural parishes and small farms, some of which were here and listed as sub-manors in the Domesday Book. By the time of Domesday, Cullompton was an important centre and the church was given by King William the Conqueror to the abbey he founded at Battle in thanks for his victory at Hastings (it later passed to St Nicholas Priory in Exeter). The church at that time was already wealthy, with five holdings, and this suggests that it was a Saxon minster; such minsters were the centre of the wider Christian community with responsibility for teaching, and were often the only places where baptisms took place.

71 ST GEORGE'S WELL

Grid Reference: ST023084. Good public access to general area.

In 1317 a Charter from the Abbot of Buckfast granted a fair on the Feast of St George at Cullompton, and the celebrations from that time have been centred on a field to the east of the town where a map of 1765 shows St George's Well. Today the field is still intact having escaped the development (including a St George's Well Close) which has taken place all around. A number of natural

St George's Well.

drains and springs migrate along the field but local enquiries failed to say which is St George's Well.

Traditional Uses: Cure for problems of the eye.

Parish: Shobrooke
Ordnance Survey Explorer Map 114

A visit to Shobrooke is a must for anyone who wants to see the best of Mid Devon's cob country. A third of all the buildings in the parish are listed as being of architectural importance and many of these are built from cob, based on the local red earth. Not all of the cob is ancient however; in 2002 a local project was funded to carry out repairs to the cob wall around the churchyard and this was done as a community task involving local people and the re-learning of the skill of cob building under expert tuition. The parish church is an ancient building dedicated to St Swithin but has been dedicated to Thomas à Becket and Peter in the past.

72 HOLY WELL
Grid Reference: SS863012. Good public access; the well is set in a hedge-bank a hundred yards or so from the church past Shobrooke Barton Farm.

This little well was restored in 1925 but is of ancient origins. The earliest record is in the church accounts of 1576 'paid for making clene of the Well and pavynge, 20 shillings'. Local pride in the Holy Well is still maintained today and a short time of worship is held beside it on Ascension Day.

Traditional Uses: Baptismal use.

Parish: Bow
Ordnance Survey Explorer Map 113

The original name for this parish was Nymet Tracey. Nymet from the Celtic word for sacred grove and Tracey from the family of that name who lived here in the 12th century (Sir William de Tracey was one of the knights who took part in the murder of Thomas à Becket in 1170). Today the village at Bow

Holy Well.

Puddock's Well.

stands some way from the parish church of St Bartholomew but at one time there was a sizable hamlet at Nymet Tracey towards the site of the de Tracey manor which was located near Hilldown. The many Nymet place names in the parish and its proximity to the Roman road and fort at North Tawton are a reminder that this was the centre of a complex of places sacred to the tribes of pre-Christian Dumnonia. A significant Roman garrison was needed at the fort to ensure that those visiting the sacred groves and waters did not pose a threat to the route westwards. You can join the Two Moors Way near here or follow the network of lanes and paths to Nymet and Beer sacred grove places.

73 PUDDOCK'S WELL

Grid Reference: SS731006. Good public access; the well is in a depression below where the road widens slightly and near the parish church towards Walson Barton.

The spring is underneath an ancient oak tree below the level of the road, and the cistern which catches the water is concealed by a flimsy corrugated iron cover (beware and do not stand on it as it is often covered by leaves). The name of the well is a mystery; possibly a Celtic priest Puttoc or even Petroc; puttock in Old English meant marshy ground, or a buzzard. The road broadens here to take account of the site of the well and it is most likely that this place has some connection with the sacred grove tradition of the area.

Traditional Uses: Lost.

Parish: Cheldon
Ordnance Survey Explorer Map 127

This is one of the parishes close to the valleys of the Rivers Taw and Little Dart which are such excellent and little-explored parts of Devon. It is a small parish of 1099 acres. The nearby woodlands of Eggesford Forest and the walking routes along the Tarka Trail and the Ridge and Valley Walk, take you through varied scenery in a rural landscape where wildlife is plentiful (although the roe deer in this area are hunted by one of the few remaining packs of buckhounds) and through farms and villages which have stood here since Anglo-Saxons cleared the wildwood. The church is St Mary's and a Christian place of worship has stood here since the 12th century.

74 CHURCH HOUSE WELL

Grid Reference: SS734135. Good public access; the well is by the road-side on a corner opposite the church.

Church House Well.

Tucked into the roadside hedge are the remains of a stone and slate structure which once covered a well and possibly the village pump. In 1859 the Church House on this corner was occupied by 'poor people' and the garden was let for 10 shillings to support them; this well was used by the occupants of the Church House and by the church.

Traditional Uses: Lost.

Other Parishes:

Some other places in Mid Devon where there are traditions of a Holy Well or references to wells of ancient lineage:

Bampton – Chalybeate (iron rich) well in Frog Street.

Burlescombe – well at site of 12th century Cannonsleigh Abbey.

Clannaborough – St Petroc's Well; warm water good for eyes.

Colebrook – St Mary's Well; a large well where there is a legend of a lady on horseback falling into it.

Cruwys Morchard – Holy Cross Well in the grounds of Cruwys Morchard House.

Lapford – Holy Well cure for eyes.

Morebath – St Sidwell's Well; place name evidence halegwell possibly in grounds of the old vicarage.

Silverton – water source which is good for eye problems.

St Mary's Church from the well.

NORTH DEVON DISTRICT

Parish: Rackenford
Ordnance Survey Explorer Map 114

This is a Saxon village and the name probably means 'settlement with two fording places' which suggests that this has always been a rather damp place (an 18th century vicar found the winters here so harsh that he decamped to Tiverton). Standing between Tiverton and South Molton, the fortunes of Rackenford have largely been linked to farming and the cattle markets which were held here until the Second World War. There are still extensive tracts of moorland in this area and they are important habitats for several rare plant and bird species.

Holy Trinity Well.

75 HOLY TRINITY WELL
Grid Reference: SX851183. Good public access; the site of the well is on rough unenclosed land near the church.

The 15th century parish church is dedicated to All Saints but was originally Holy Trinity. Within living memory a well which had retained the original name of the church stood close by, surrounded by a low stone wall and covered with a thatched roof. Unfortunately all trace of this has gone and it is now not possible to determine which of the several springs here was the source for the Holy Well.

Traditional Uses: Curative for problems of the eye.

Parish: North Molton
Ordnance Survey Explorer Map OL9

North Molton lies on the borders of Exmoor and it is a good base from which to explore the southern edge of the National Park. The history of the parish has a number of surprises: mining for gold was tried here in the 19th century and there is still controversy about whether this scheme was promoted as a way of extracting money from foolish shareholders, or if the levels of gold to be found in the ores were indeed sufficient to provide a return on investments. The Williams family from Cornwall operated a copper mine in the parish from 1801 to about 1860, and the miners and their families who were attracted here made North Molton a lively place, especially on Fair days which were held three times each year. One of the Fairs was a Parish Revel connected with celebrations on Ascension Day at the Holy Well. The Revel seems to have been a jolly affair with a fairground and donkey-cart rides from the village. The last recorded Revel was held in 1912.

76 HOLY WELL
Grid Reference: SS766315. On private farmland land and no public access.

The Revel at North Molton was known throughout the area and at its heart was always the Holy Well. A report from the *North Devon Herald* of 1884 explained 'On Thursday Last, Ascension Day, this celebrated well was as usual visited by suffering mortals with various disease. One lady came from Tiverton…' The custom was for the flagstone bottom of the 20-inch deep well to be cleaned out before Holy Thursday and, when visited by sufferers, they were expected to throw silver money into the well. Some visitors were so anxious to have the first chance of bathing their eyes or drinking the water at daybreak that they used to arrive the previous evening. At the end of Ascension Day the coins thrown into the water would be carefully scooped out by a 'a long handled bowl made for the purpose.'

Holy Well.

With such recent recorded use it is especially disappointing to find the tradition now entirely lost. The site of the well is not well known and has become so neglected that it has virtually disappeared, with no sign of the flagstone basin which used to be cleaned out so carefully.

Leading to the well there are signs of an old trackway through the field to where, in the early 19th century, it was reported there was still evidence of a small building standing; this may have been the Holywell Chapel of Ease licensed in the 14th century.

Track to Holy Well.

This is a Holy Well where it would be a wonderful community project to restore the site and to obtain access to it once again.

Traditional Uses: Problems of the eyes and general healing properties.

Parish: Romansleigh
Ordnance Survey Explorer Map 127

Do try and visit Romansleigh (or Rumonsleigh as it perhaps should be called). It is a tiny village which stands on a hill overlooking the tributaries of the River Mole, and it has just a few cottages and the church of St Rumon. This was one of the 15 manors held by Tavistock Abbey at the time of the Domesday Book at which time it was simply called Liege. The village and church seem to have taken their name from the patron saint of that abbey which was founded in AD974 and dedicated to Mary and St Rumon. When William of Malmsbury visited Tavistock Abbey in 1120 he wrote that 'Rumon lies there buried as a Bishop, decorated with a beautiful shrine but there are no written records to confirm the traditions about him.' Despite the lack of records at that time, we can be certain that Rumon's remains had been brought to Tavistock from Ruan Lanihorne in Cornwall. It is possible that at some time later parts of his body were sent elsewhere as holy relics (this was a fairly common practice in the 12th and 13th centuries); Glastonbury Abbey is recorded as having relics of St Rumon. Perhaps Rumonsleigh also shared in the distribution of holy relics from the saint.

77 ST RUMON'S WELL
Grid Reference: SS727205. Good public access; the well lies just outside the churchyard hedge.

This little well-house was renovated and then re-dedicated by the Bishop of Exeter in 1959 and is a simple stone structure now covered with ivy, standing just outside the northern churchyard boundary hedge. A few shallow steps lead down to the water which seems to come from a spring at the bottom of the well basin.

Traditional Uses: Baptisms.

St Rumon's Well.

Parish: Chittlehampton
Ordnance Survey Explorer Map 127

Of all the parishes in Devonshire, it is Chittlehampton where the importance of a saint and her Holy Well are still best remembered and celebrated. The village was here at the time of Saxons (the name means 'settlement in the hollow') but it is the events which happened to a local girl from nearby Stowford which made Chittlehampton famous. Legend tells us that in the 6th century, St Urith (or St Hieritha – an Anglicised version of her name or St Teara – a local version) lived at nearby Stowford and that she was converted to Christianity, possibly by monks from Glastonbury. The date suggests that she was probably a native Celt and less likely to have been an Anglo-Saxon as this area was only colonised towards the end of that century. Her new-found faith was blamed for a drought and her stepmother persuaded local farmers to kill the girl; they did this by cutting off her head with a scythe. At the place where she died, a spring of pure water sprang up, scarlet pimpernels blossomed where spots of her blood fell, and divine vengeance fell on her murderers.

This story contains familiar elements of a beheading of a Christian believer. A spring of water and miracles are also found in the legends of St Sidwell of Exeter, St Nectan of Stoke and St Juthwara of Sherborne. Eventually St Urith's remains were buried in the church at Chittlehampton and this, and her Holy Well, became the focus for pilgrimages. The value of the gifts left by grateful pilgrims exceeded even those left at Exeter Cathedral and St Michael's Mount in Cornwall. When her image and shrine was removed from the church after the Reformation in 1538, the loss of income from these gifts was such that the vicar appealed against the assessment of his income, and saying that he needed more compensation for loss of earnings! No record of the healing miracles performed by St Urith has survived but we know what could happen at such shrines from an eye-witness account of 1113, from St Petroc's at Bodmin:

...a certain girl of about 10 years of age, who was blind from birth, having bathed her eyes with water in which the relics of the Saint had been washed, forthwith received her sight. There was also a deaf youth in the town who washed his ears with the water and straightway recovered.

The importance of the cult of St Urith is supported by a hymn to her which was found in a 15th century book from Glastonbury Abbey. There seem to be two slightly different translations from the Latin:

Day by day the morning's rays,
Ever utter to God's praise
Urith's undying fame.
Here in everlasting grace she grew,
Modest, comely, good and true.
Here all virtues crowned her name.

And:
Daily the morning's ray, tell out to God his praise.
And freshly shine on Urith's holy fame.
Twas here her maiden dower, grew fragrant like a flower,
And here her faith burned steady as flame.

There where the maiden fell, gushed forth a healing well,
A stream of pardon foe her kinsfold's hate;
And there the parched earth, bore flowers to hide its dearth.
Fair tribute to her faith inviolate.

Sing Chittlehampton, sing! Let All Devon's meadows ring
With holy gladness foe our Saviour's renown!
And thou, blest maiden, pray, that we in this our day
May bear our cross and win our crown.

Icon of St Urith.

The legacy of St Urith and the pilgrims who honoured her are remembered by one of the finest church buildings in Devon, with its statue of the saint on the tower and by the parishioners on her day (8 July) with a service and blessing at her Holy Well. A unique Devonshire celebration which deserves more recognition and support.

78 ST URITH'S WELL

Grid Reference: SS637255. Good public access; the well is just a little way from the church along a narrow lane near Rose Cottage.

St Urith's Well.

The well has been much renovated, most recently by local authorities, including the North Devon Water Board; they did not do justice to such an important site. The well itself was covered by an iron manhole cover and the ancient stone slab, with its carved shallow trough from which pilgrims touched the water, was set in an an ugly concrete surround. It deserves better and there are plans for improvement.

Traditional Uses: Healing and blessings.

Parish: Tawstock
Ordnance Survey Explorer Map 139

Tawstock overlooks the River Taw and although it is not far from the bustling streets of Barnstaple, it has the air of a truly rural parish. At the time of the Domesday Book, it was one of the far-flung manors held by the king; it later passed to Judhael of Totnes and then over the centuries through various families to the Wreys until the estate was sold in the 1970s. The fine house at Tawstock Court replaced an Elizabethan mansion which was burnt down in 1787 (the medieval gatehouse remains near the church) and today it is a preparatory school. The parish church close to the school is dedicated to St Peter, and the Holy Well is also known as St Peter's Well.

79 ST PETER'S WELL

Grid Reference: SS553298. Good public access; the well is on the roadside next to the village primary school.

This well is mentioned as halghewille – Holy Well – in 1390 and today the large well-house, which was renovated in 1938, stands in the shade of two

St Peter's Well.

large yew trees. Inside, the well-house has a grotto-like appearance and a pool of clear water. The parish church has no recent record of the water being used for baptisms and the only local legend is that the site is close to an ancient oak tree known as 'Saxon Oak'.

Traditional Uses: Lost.

Parishes: Horwood and Westleigh
Ordnance Survey Explorer Map 139

These neighbouring parishes lie close to the estuary of the River Torridge but the villages are bypassed by the traffic making its way to Bideford, Barnstaple and to the sands at Instow. Much of the village of Westleigh was occupied by estate workers working at nearby Tapley Park, and this interesting cluster of cob and thatched houses is situated so that none of the cottages is visible from the 'big house'. Tapley Park is part of the Christie Estate which owns most of the foreshore on both sides of the estuary; the grand gardens are open to the public and have splendid walks with views of the river.

80 ST MICHAEL'S WELL
Grid Reference: SS500283. On private farmland (but close to a level public footpath).

St Michael's Well.

In the middle of a field behind the parish church, a startled hare with eyes staring and ears back, bounded away from me as I approached a large overgrown gully from where a trickle of water seeps from a spring. This is the only remaining evidence for this ancient Holy Well which takes its name from the church which has been dedicated to St Michael the Archangel since at least 1386. In times past the well was much resorted to by local people and it is sad that today it seems only to be a dumping ground for bits of old concrete and agricultural debris.

Traditional Uses: A cure for eye problems and 'eruptions'.

81 ST PETROC'S WELL

Grid Reference: SS473286. On private farmland (but close to a level public footpath).

This Holy Well lies in a field across the road from the parish church which has been dedicated to St Peter since 1740; some references suggest that prior to this it was to St Petroc. Local stories say the well has never been known to run dry and this was supported by the current landowner. Above ground there is very little evidence of the well apart from an old style agricultural pump which takes water for livestock. The landowner in 2003 was not at all keen to provide information about the well 'in case people want to visit it'. A public footpath across the field passes close to the well site.

St Petroc's Well.

Traditional Uses: Lost.

Parish: Pilton
Ordnance Survey Explorer Map 139

Although now almost swallowed by Barnstaple, Pilton has a longer history than its larger neighbour and still retains the character of the settlement which grew up around the Benedictine Priory established here by King Athelstan in the 10th century. The handsome parish church of St Mary the Virgin stands at the top of the main street and amongst the many interesting features inside is a carving of a 'Green Man', the ancient symbol of nature and fertility. There was a leper hospital here in medieval times. Pilton also has a legend of a sea monster 'The Pilton Worm' which was seen in the estuary near where the River Yeo joins the estuary of the Taw.

Ladywell.

82 LADYWELL

Grid Reference: SS556344. Good public access; the well is in a little lane behind the parish church.

A small arched recess protected by a metal grill sits in the wall of the lane and receives water from the spring. Renovation work was carried out in the 1980s and this Holy Well then had the unusual distinction of being blessed by a senior member of the Orthodox Church, Metropolitan Anthony of Sourozh. This was a splendid ceremony of blessing which was attended by several hundred people and is perhaps the most recent example of an ancient Holy Well in Devon being re-dedicated to its proper status.

Traditional Uses: Baptisms and healing.

Parish: Braunton
Ordnance Survey Explorer Map 139

This is an important parish alongside the great Taw–Torridge estuaries and there are many reasons to spend some time here. Braunton has one of the very few remaining examples of a medieval open field system left in England; known as the Great Field, it is a low-lying area of some 350 acres, close to the estuary, with a unique pattern of field strips and old barns. The village is named after St Brannoc, a Celtic Saint who arrived from Wales in the 6th century, and whose cult was one of the few in Devon to survive. There was a Saxon minster at Braunton and a number of ancient chapels in the parish were probably associated with this central foundation; records suggest that there were chapels dedicated to St Gregory, St Anne, St Sylvester and St Michael. Both the current Anglican and Roman Catholic churches in Braunton are dedicated to St Brannoc. To add to the confusion, a legend tells that St Brannoc tried to build his first church on nearby Chapel Hill (the ruins here are those of St Michael's Chapel) but each night the devil carried all the stones to the bottom again. Eventually, the saint decided to place his church on the spot where a dream had told him he would find a sow and seven piglets. The life of St Brannoc is given in a medieval manuscript held by the British Museum and tells how the saint owned a great cow which was guarded by a wolf; St Brannoc's cow was slaughtered by the local lord and the wolf ran to tell his master what had happened. Meanwhile the cow had been skinned, cut up and put into a large cooking pot, but the water would not boil. The local lord realised that St Brannoc's power was great and so he prayed for forgiveness; the saint called the cow from the pot, whereupon it reassembled itself. This legend is similar to that of St Nectan and the eel told at Stoke (Well 2) and contains symbolism which it is now difficult for us to understand.

83 ST BRANNOC'S WELL

Grid Reference: SS487374. Good public access; the well is in the grounds of St Brannoc's Roman Catholic Church.

We do not know where St Brannoc found his sow and seven piglets which a dream told him would show him where to build his church, but near the present Roman Catholic church which was built in 1957, there were the ruins of an ancient chapel. St Brannoc's Holy Well is here and is a large stone-lined pool set amongst ferns and overhanging trees below a steep hillside on which stands a statue of Our Lady. It has been described as Devon's Lourdes, and while it does not have the healing fame of that shrine, it is a place of deep peace and calm.

Traditional Uses: Baptisms.

Above: *Icon of St Brannoc.*
Left: *St Brannoc's Well.*

Parish: Georgham
Ordnance Survey Explorer Map 139

This parish is best known for the wonderful beaches at Croyde and Putsborough, and also because Henry Williamson, the author of *Tarka the Otter*, lived in Georgham and is buried in the churchyard. The Tarka Trail provides excellent walks along the coast path.

St Helen's Well.

84 ST HELEN'S WELL

Grid Reference: SS445392. Good public access; the well is down a little lane near the cottages on the site of St Helen's Chapel at Croyde.

St Helen's Chapel was a daughter-house to the Benedictine Priory at nearby Pilton and the remains have been built into a cottage here. There is some debate about the identity of St Helen as some authorities believe she was a Celtic Saint, others say she is the martyr of that name from 12th century Sweden. Most now accept that St Helen, or Helena, was the mother of Constantine, the Roman Emperor who recognised Christianity as an official religion. St Helena, from the time of her conversion around 320BC, founded a number of churches throughout the Roman Empire including in Rome and the Holy Land. There are churches dedicated to St Helen in Devon including across the bay from Croyde at Abbotsham, on Lundy and in Cornwall including chapels near Land's End and on the Isles of Scilly. The little well-house is in excellent condition and the spring which feeds it is one of a number which break along the spring-line here.

Traditional Uses: Lost.

Parish: Mortehoe
Ordnance Survey Explorer Map 139

This is another coastal parish and Morte Bay is well known for the sands at Woolacombe. As well as the popular beaches, this parish provides some wonderful cliff and inland walks, and the wells described in this parish are a good illustration of how it is possible to find secret places even in the most visited parts of Devon.

85 EYEWELL

Grid Reference: SS448455. Good public access; on National Trust Morte Point walking is a little uneven.

The tiny spring denoting Eyewell.

This is a dripping spring which is set into the slope of the land which runs down to the cliffs overlooking Morte Point. It has an

'otherworld' atmosphere and stepping into the green light of the open cave is like taking a stride away from this world and towards a place where the spirit of the earth is close.

Traditional Uses: Cures for eye problems.

86 ST JOHN'S HOLY WELL

Grid Reference: SS484415. Good public access; the well is in Chapel Wood, a nature reserve managed by the Royal Society for the Protection of Birds, and approached by an uneven but level path.

St John's Holy Well.

The well is next to the ruins of a chantry chapel dedicated to St John. The chapel dates from c.1250 and was endowed by the holder of the nearby Spreacombe manor for a priest to chant masses and prayers for his family; a two-roomed dwelling for the priest was attached to the chapel. The spring which fills the well rises under the altar of the chapel. In some ways this place is like the chantry chapel and well of ill omen at Lidwell (Well 56) but here the atmosphere is positive and hopeful. This was a Domesday manor called Sprecome, and even older is the nearby Iron Age fort.

Traditional Uses: Lost.

Parish: Lee
Ordnance Survey Explorer Map 139

This ecclesiastical parish was created in 1869 with responsibility for an area which was previously in Mortehoe and Ilfracombe. There was a Chapel of Ease mentioned here in 1416, and in 1439 as the Chapel of St Wardred at Legh; but who was this saint? St Wardrede is not shown in any Calendar of Saints and, although it has been suggested that he/she was a Celtic Saint of the 6th century, there is no evidence to support this (a link with Tywardreath in Cornwall has also been mooted but the church there is St Andrew's and the name is Cornish meaning 'House on the Sand'). Lee is just the place to expect to find a Celtic settlement and Holy Well, so perhaps a St Wardrede did come here to this most beautiful valley where the climate provides an ideal habitat for a profusion of wildflowers and fuchsia bushes.

Above: *St Wardrede's Well.*
Right: *Lee grotto.*

87 ST WARDREDE'S WELL, LEE
Grid Reference: SS485463. Good public access; alongside the road down into Lee.

Two wells are marked on the Ordnance Survey map on the right-hand side of the road down towards Lee; one of these is where water from a spring trickles down a tumble of rocks which seems to be a man-made grotto, and the second is a little stone structure set into the bank at Chapel Cottage. The cottage is believed to be the site of the Chapel of Ease mentioned in the 15th century and which may have been dedicated by the Champernown family who were patrons of Ilfracombe and also had connections with Tywardreath.

Traditional Uses: Lost.

Parish: Parracombe
Ordnance Survey Explorer Map OL9

St Petroc's church, Parracombe.

The main A39 road from Barnstaple swings in a great arc around the village of Parracombe but it would be a mistake to pass it by. The name Parracombe is often taken to be a corruption of 'Petroc's Coombe' but this is probably not correct and it may be Anglo-Saxon for 'valley with an enclosure'. It is an ancient place which has been occupied since before the coming of the Normans. It has an earthworks called Holwell Castle and a famous 13th-century church dedicated to St Petroc. Of the castle very little is known; the manor here was held at the time of Domesday by William of Falaise and the motte and bailey fortifications are typical of early defensive sites. St Petroc's Church stands a little way from the village (in a 'Churchtown' which is also the pattern for many Celtic foundations in Cornwall and Brittany), and is of particular interest because the interior has changed little for the past 200 years. In 1879 it was proposed to demolish the church and build a new one on the site; there was an outcry from the admirers of ancient buildings (including

John Ruskin). As a result the old church was left standing and a new church, Christ Church, was erected closer to the village.

88 LADY'S WELL

Grid Reference: SS678448. Good public access; the well is adjacent to a public footpath which is the old trackway route from the village to Parracombe Common.

A small, low 19th or 20th-century brick built well-head with a metal cover stands under an ash tree next to the track and its appearance is consistent with this being the source of water which still supplies two cottages in the Churchtown. Two of these cottages were once the church house where ale was brewed to refresh worshippers at St Petroc's Church, and who may have travelled across the moor to get here. The dedication as Lady's Well suggests a medieval date.

Traditional Uses: Lost.

Above: *Lady's Well.*
Below: *St Thomas's Well.*

89 ST THOMAS'S WELL

Grid Reference: SS676451. No public access; on private land.

This spring is close to St Petroc's Church, in a steep gully lying below the main A39 road. In the 19th century it was used to supply water to the

village and in 1952 the old collecting tanks were modernised by the North Devon Water Board. The site was further developed in 1995 when a supply of up to 1000 cubic metres of water each week was needed for the village. St Thomas's Well no longer provides the water supply but the collecting tanks remain on the site. Drawings made for the 1952 modernisation show that there were several springs at this spot which, despite the intrusion of the modern workings and proximity to the road, still has a special feeling.

Traditional Uses: Lost.

Water Board drawing of St Thomas's springs.

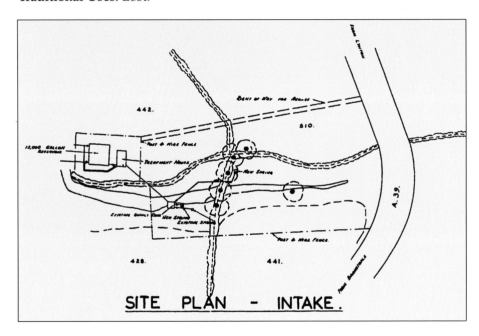

Parish: Lynton
Ordnance Survey Explorer Map OL9

In the Exmoor National Park, Lynton is at the mouth of the steep valley of the River Lyn which rushes through woodland and down to the sea. The Two Moors Way ends, or begins, at Lynton and it is an ideal place from which to explore Exmoor.

90 LADYWELL
Grid Reference: SS712491. On private land.

Ladywell.

This spring is close to the Valley of the Rocks and overlooks Lynton and the sea beyond. It is set in a wooded coombe and the plentiful pure water from the spring was once used as a water supply for Lynton. The reason for the name Ladywell is unknown and although the parish church is dedicated to Mary, this is not an ancient title. Ladywell is a dedication often associated with medieval wells and suggests that this is a place which has been visited for many hundreds of years.

Traditional Uses: Lost.

Parish: Countisbury
Ordnance Survey Explorer Map OL9

This pilgrimage to the Holy Wells of Devon began at Athelstan's boundary with Cornwall and by crossing into Welcombe on the Atlantic coast; it ends at the boundary with Somerset on the coast of the Bristol Channel. At Welcombe we were in a wild, windswept landscape and here at Countisbury the sweep of Exmoor is at our back and the steep oakwoods stretch before us down to the sea. Since the time of the Romans this has been a strategic place; a small fortlet was built here at the head of the Coscombe valley as its position gave it commanding views over the sea towards Wales and up the coast to Porlock and beyond. The tribes of South Wales had offered strong resistance to the Romans and an attack from them across the Bristol Channel could not be ruled out; the Countisbury fort provided a look out and warning station. The small garrison here consisted of about 70 men and it was occupied for three or four summers; a similar fortlet was built soon after at Martinhoe, west of Lynmouth. The watch over the Severn was kept up until about AD70 or slightly later when the legion moved from Exeter to Gloucester and then to a new fortress in Wales at Caerleon.

At the mouth of the valley is a small pebbly beach; legend has it that it was at this spot where a trader called Joseph of Arimathea landed on his way to Glastonbury. To finish, or to begin at a place associated with such a pilgrim, is to share in the spirit of the place which is to be found here and at many of the other Holy Wells of Devon.

91 SISTER'S FOUNTAIN

Grid Reference: SS794492. Good public access; the well is on National Trust land beside the footpath (steep) from County Gates to Glenthorne and on to Culbone.

The Glenthorne Estate was developed in 1829 by the Rev. Walter Halliday on land above a cove which until then had only been used by local smugglers.

Sister's Fountain.

High in deep oakwoods above the cove was a spring of ever-flowing clear water; it sprang from the earth at the spot where legend says that Joseph of Arimathea struck the ground with his staff to find water to drink. The Rev. Halliday's four nieces loved this place and it was renovated and named Sister's Fountain after them.

Traditional Uses: Lost.

Other Parishes:
Some other places in North Devon where there are traditions of a Holy Well or references to wells of ancient lineage:
Bratton Fleming – Holy Well near Holy Well Wood.
Ilfracombe – two wells near Hele, one may be associated with a leper colony.
Morthoe – Lady Well behind Old Post Office.
South Molton – Eye Pits in Station Road.
Parracombe – Holwell Castle spring of St Helen.

Sister's Fountain entrance.

We shall not cease from exploration,

And the end of all our exploring

Will be to arrive where we started

And to know the place for the first time.

(T S Eliot – *The Four Quartets – Little Gidding*).

The Early Celtic Church in Devon

I have a hut in the wood, none knows it but my Lord;
an ash tree this side, a hazel on the other.
A great tree on a mound encloses it.
Two heathery door-posts for support, a lintel of honey-suckle
Around its close the wood sheds its nuts for the fat swine.
Excellent fresh springs – a cup of water; splendid drink
They gush forth abundantly; yew berries, bird cherries
Fruits of rowan, black sloes of the dark blackthorn;
Foods of whorts, spare berries, sweet apples, red hog berries... *

Devon has a wealth of ancient churches and one of the delights of exploring the county is to come across some remote village church which has witnessed the faithful worship of generations of local people. Splendid they are and although most date from the 15th–16th centuries, many incorporate parts of much older structures from the time of the Normans. In some cases, the foundations are Saxon but the evidence for this is scanty. If we try to look even further back to the time of the Celtic Saints (5th–8th centuries), then there is no part of a church remaining from that period. However, there is information to be found about Devon in the age of the saints and this is a brief introduction to a neglected aspect of spiritual history.

What was Celtic Christianity? Some historians claim that it is misleading to use the term or to talk about a Celtic Church; certainly there was no independent structure or institution which defined itself and its beliefs by excluding other Christian traditions. However there was a form of Christianity followed in the western Celtic lands, which held on to characteristics which were absent in the development of doctrine taking place in Rome. While not claiming to be a separate faith, Celtic Christianity held a distinctive approach to spirituality which flowered in Dumnonia (Cornwall, Devon and West Somerset) and the rest of the British Isles, during the first centuries which followed the ending of Roman rule.

Christianity came with the Romans and by AD410, when the legions had withdrawn, much of southern Britain had been touched by this new religion. It is

---

* adapted from the Hermit's Hut, a Celtic poem from the 10th century

133

probable that its first followers in Devon were from the few military and trading centres which had been established (there is evidence of an early-Christian cemetery near the present cathedral in Exeter). However, we should look to the so called Celtic Saints from Ireland and Wales, for the origins of the early Church in Devon. They had the most influence in spreading a particular form of Christianity which was cherished here for more than four hundred years.

Traditions about the holy men and women who arrived along the coasts of Dumnonia in the 5th and 6th centuries are widespread; they are said to have come as missionaries to spread the faith amongst the pagan native peoples. In reality many such travellers came not to teach others but primarily as pilgrims following a discipline of 'peregrinatio', sometimes known as 'the white martyr-dom' – a self-imposed wandering away from all that is familiar in search of a closeness to God. They were seeking some remote spot where they could better listen to the heartbeat of God in themselves and in the natural world around. Celtic sites are often in places which even today, are quiet and open to the influences of nature and the seasons. The saints (in the Celtic world this meant 'holy and learned') brought little with them, some did not even have a Gospel book, and they sought only a simple place to live and worship. These first settlements became many of Devon's first Christian places of worship. By their example and through the stories they told, the saints influenced the people in the countryside around and small Christian communities grew.

The teachings and spirituality of the Celtic Saints were inspired by the theology of a 4th century British Christian called Pelagius. He had a strong sense of the goodness of creation, and of God being present within all life. Pelagius rejected the doctrine of original sin and taught that everyone, men and women, could find God for themselves and need not depend only on an organised Church for spiritual counsel. He wrote:

You will realise that doctrines are inventions of the human mind, as it tries to penetrate the mystery of God. You will realise that the Scripture itself is the work of human minds, recording the example and teaching of Jesus. Thus it is not what you believe that matters; it is how you respond with your heart and your actions. It is not believing in Christ that matters, it is becoming like him...

In the year AD380, Pelagius had travelled to Rome where he became a successful teacher and where his views became highly respected by the Church authorities. His ideas began to attract popular support but he made enemies amongst powerful preachers such as Augustine of Hippo, and in AD418 the Pope was persuaded to declare him a heretic. He returned home to Britain where his teaching continued to have significant influence over much of later Celtic spirituality. The sense of wonder for the natural world which is present in many Celtic prayers was first given voice in another of the writings of Pelagius:

Look at the animals roaming the forest; God's spirit dwells in them. Look at the birds flying across the sky; God's spirit dwells in them. Look at the fish in the river and the sea; God's spirit dwells in them... When God pronounced his creation was good, it was not only that his hand had fashioned every creature; it was that his breath had brought every creature to life. Look too at the great trees of the forest; look at the wild flowers and the grass in the fields...

This is a flavour of the early Celtic Church which existed in Devon – a tradition which has left little in the way of permanent memorials but which still has much to enrich our own times and lives. Clues about its presence do remain and there are a number of possible sources of information.

Lives of the Saints

The Lives of the Saints were mostly written very many years after the events they describe. They are not reliable as history and indeed may never have been intended to be read as such. Instead in story form, they give insights into the spiritual and the actual journeys, made by the men and women who spread Celtic Christianity in Dumnonia:

- **St Nectan c.AD468–510:** according to his Life (written in the 12th century), St Nectan was one of the twenty-four sons and daughters of King Brychan of Breconshire, all of whom travelled to Devon and Cornwall on voyages of peregrinatio (in Celtic Christianity, everyone is a child of God and so they may have been Brychan's spiritual family rather than his earthly children). Nectan settled at Stoke, near Hartland, close to a spring of pure water. Through his example, many local people converted to the Christian faith. Some years after arriving at Stoke, Nectan was set upon by robbers and beheaded. His Life tells how his faith was so strong that he was able to pick up his head and carry it 'half a league' to his Holy Well; a stone there was said to show stains of his blood for many centuries. Following this miracle, a church was built to house the saint's body and it became a place of pilgrimage where 'sight was restored to the blind, hearing to the deaf and speech to the dumb.' A Celtic monastic community grew up around Stoke and the canons from there tended a number of holdings and chapels in Hartland Hundred.

Some 500 years after St Nectan's death, the then Saxon Bishop of Crediton did not believe in the miracles credited to this Celtic Saint but the Life tells how he was forced to accept the holiness of St Nectan when the body of the saint was exhumed, and 'so sweet and fragrant an odour arose that it was as if all the spices and perfumes of the world were shut up in that sepulchre. A brilliant light shone from heaven, dazzling the eyes of all that were present.' The cult of St Nectan was one of the few Celtic traditions in Devon which was accepted by the Saxon and later the English Church.

- **St Brannoc:** this saint arrived at Braunton some time around AD581 but much about him remains a mystery. There is no extant Life, but traditions tell how he devoted himself to teaching local people about farming and in particular the use of natural fertilizers to enrich the soil (the first organic farmer). St Brannoc yoked wild deer to work for him and stories tell how he had a tame wolf which would drive the saint's milk cow to pasture. These tales are similar to those told about another Celtic Saint, St Brynach of Wales, and it has been suggested that the two saints are one and the same. The strength of St Brannoc's cult makes it certain that the saint did actually live and work at Braunton. As the importance of the community founded by St Brannoc began to increase, it is possible that some of the St Brynach stories were attached to it to add to its authority. Already a powerful cult when the Saxon's moved into North Devon, it became a wealthy 'minster' which later formed part of the endowment for the Deanery of Exeter. Although the details of St Brannoc's life are obscure, his cult was another of the very few Celtic traditions from Devon which was accepted by the Church in later times.

- **St Paul Aurelian (Paul de Leon):** in AD508 it is recorded that this monk from Wales travelled across Devon and Cornwall, where his sister St Wulvella lived (she is known at Ashburton as St Gudula), before crossing into Brittany where he was consecrated a bishop in AD516.

- **St Sampson:** this saint's Life is one of the earliest still surviving (it was written in AD620). It tells how in AD527 this bishop from Wales landed at Padstow, North Cornwall. He then journeyed to Lewannick near Launceston and possibly towards the River Tamar at Bradstone (where tradition says that the family of St David had settled) before ridding the countryside of a serpent and going on to Dol in Brittany.

- **St Petroc:** although Petroc is known as the foremost of Cornish Saints, his influence was widespread, including those parts of Dumnonia which became Devon when King Athelston fixed the boundary in AD927. There were at least 18 churches dedicated to St Petroc in Devon (see table overleaf) and others in Somerset, Wales and Brittany. Relics, including his clothes, hair and a bone were held in Exeter Cathedral (Bodmin Priory, Glastonbury and Waltham Abbey also had some bones of St Petroc). In AD575, the saint travelled in Cornwall and Devon, and events took place at Newton St Petroc that led him to go on a pilgrimage to Rome. The story is told in Chapter 2.

- **St Sidwell and St Urith:** the cult of St Sidwell was already established in Exeter at the end of the 7th century, around the time when the Saxons first occupied the area. In 1300 a Life of the Saint was included in Bishop Grandisson's documents at Exeter Cathedral and by this time she was claimed to be a Saxon rather than a Celtic maiden. The legend of a holy virgin who was beheaded and of a spring of pure water issuing from the ground where she fell, is also found in the Life of St Urith of Chittlehampton. This story has parallels in Celtic mythology and the early date for these two established local Devon traditions does indicate that they were existing cults which were later taken over by the Saxon Church.

- **St Wenn:** this 5th-century saint was another of King Brychan's children who travelled to Devon and settled, close to her brother Nectan, at Cheristow in Hartland. Very little is known about St Wenn (sometimes called St Wenna) but in addition to her church at Cheristow, there were dedications to her in Cornwall and a Holy Well at Trenant near Wadebridge.

Church Dedications

Throughout Devon there are churches which have, or once had, a dedication to a Celtic Saint (see map on page 139). The practice of dedicating a permanent church building to a patron saint began in the 4th century but despite this, many churches remained without a recorded patron into the 13th century. In the Middle Ages, some 30 per cent of Devon's churches did not have an official patron; it is likely that some of these had been Celtic foundations for which the local traditions had been lost or were ignored by the Saxon and English ecclesiastical authorities.

Dedication to a particular saint may have been because of some local connection, as a result of the influence of the bishop who was responsible for the ceremony, or even a misunderstanding of earlier traditions; for example St Petroc was sometimes read as St Patrick, and some dedications stem from a guess based on the date when the parish feast day was once celebrated. Changes of patron also took place and so an ancient site which now has a patron from the mainstream of church tradition, does not rule out an earlier Celtic connection. Equally, caution must be exercised when attributing a present day Celtic dedication as evidence for a link with the pre-Saxon Church (see table below).

The following table gives some clues about possible Celtic Church locations:

Dates when Celtic Church dedications were first recorded.

Before 1086		Before 1600		After 1600	
Place	*Dedication*	*Place*	*Dedication*	*Place*	*Dedication*
St Budeaux	St Budoc	West Worlington	St Petroc	Staverton	St Paul de Leon
Petrocstowe	St Petroc	West Anstey	St Petroc	Newton St Cyres	St Juliot
Newton St Petroc	St Petroc	Welcombe	St Nectan	Inwardleigh	St Petroc
Landkey	St Key (Cei)	Virginstowe	St Bridget	Dunkeswell	St Petroc
Instow	John?	Torre	St Petroc	Brendon	St Brendon
Hartland	St Nectan	South Brent	St Petroc		
Exeter	St Sidwell	Romansleigh	St Rumon		
Coryton	St Curig	Parracombe	St Petroc		
Chittlehampton	St Urith	Lydford	St Petroc		
Cheristow	St Wenn	Lewtrenchard	St Petroc		
Bridestowe	St Bridget	Hollacombe	St Petroc		
Braunton	St Brannoc	Harpford	St Petroc		
Bradstone	St Nonna	Farringdon	St Petroc		
		Ashton	St Nectan		
		Clannaborough	St Petroc		
		Cotleigh	St Petroc		
		Dartmouth	St Petroc		
		East Portlemouth	St Winwalloe		
		Exeter	St Kerrian		
		Exeter	St Petroc		

Churches dedicated to Celtic Saints

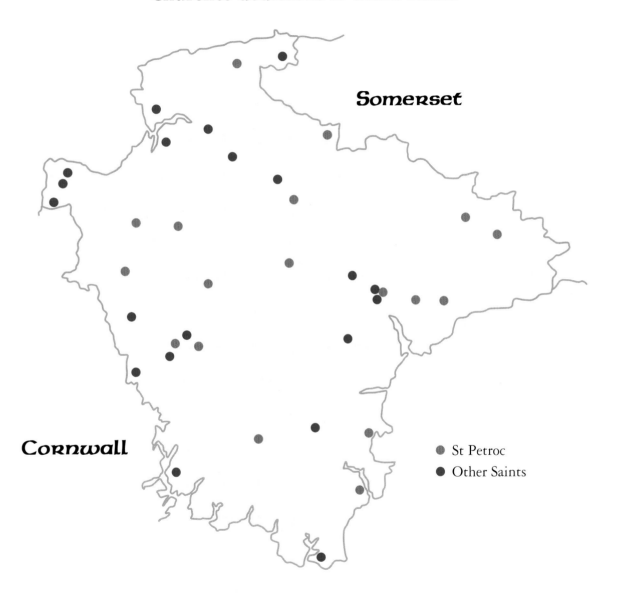

Above: *St Petroc's, West Anstey.*
Right: *St Petroc's, Hollacombe.*

Place name and physical evidence

The Celtic words llan or lann, described a holy place and are usually associated with an oval or circular area enclosed by a bank or wall which is higher than the surrounding land. Such enclosures mark a Celtic Christian cemetery and probably the associated place of worship. Landcross, Landkey and Clannaborough are lann sites. Although the Celtic descriptive words have been lost, the shape of a lann site has also been identified at: Stowford (near Okehampton), Lustleigh and Lydford.

(Coryton appears as llancurig in a Saxon document but there is no evidence remaining of circular enclosure).

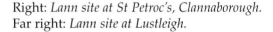

Right: *Lann site at St Petroc's, Clannaborough.*
Far right: *Lann site at Lustleigh.*

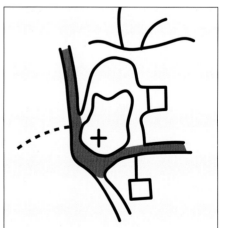

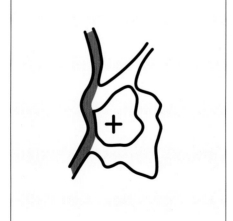

Celtic place names in Devon are rare and this is an indication of the extent to which the original culture was replaced by the Saxons who moved east in the 7th century. Despite this, the local population held on to many of its Celtic Christian traditions until the 9th or 10th centuries. Church buildings of that time were made of wood or cob, and none have survived; there are however a few special standing stones which date from the earliest days of the Celtic Church. About a dozen of these stones have been identified so far. They came from the 5th to the 9th centuries and were seemingly erected as memorials to someone who had recently died. Most have vertical carved letters which are now difficult to make out but they seem to be inscriptions in Latin and some contain personal names. The stone at Stowford (also a lann site) has the curious word GURGLES.

Nearby at Sourton, it has been suggested that the words on the 6th century stone are PRINCIPI VIRIVCI AUDETI, and at Tavistock a stone memorial of similar age reads DOBUNI FABII FILI ENABARRUS. At Parracombe the wording on the standing stone is CAVUDI FILIUS CIVILI.

Far left: *Stowford Stone.*
Left: *Sourton Stone.*

Opposite: Clannaborough church.

We do not know why these standing stone memorials were erected, or who they commemorated, but it is most likely that they were people of high status and who were associated with some of the first Christian communities in Devon.

The evidence for the early Celtic Church in Devon is not plentiful but there is enough to demonstrate that it did flourish here. The stories of the Celtic Saints and their Church are often difficult for us to understand as they use imagery in ways which mean little to us. However, we should not underestimate the strength of the faith which they held. It was a spirituality which valued all creation and saw the breath of God in all things and in all people. The faith of the Celtic Church was rooted in the wonders of the world of nature and in the belief that everyone was born with essential goodness. It did not have a central authority and did not seek to be separated from other Christians but, in the end, it was pushed aside by those who saw the need for greater conformity and control over doctrine.

Celtic Christianity has been described as the Christianity We Lost. It was not lost but has been hidden, and is only now being rediscovered, not least in the spirit of place still to be found at its holy places in the countryside of Devon.

In summer with its pleasant, abundant mantle, with good tasting saviour
There are pignuts, wild marjoram, the cresses of the stream-green purity!
Swarms of bees, beetles, soft music of the world, a gentle humming;
Fair white birds come, cranes, seagulls, the sea sings to them.
Though you delight in your own enjoyments, greater than wealth, for my part
I am grateful for what is given to me...
*Grateful to the Prince who gives every good to me in my hut...** *

* adapted from the Hermit's Hut, a Celtic poem from the 10th century

Bibliography of the main sources which have been used throughout the Book

Title	Author	Publisher/date
Age of Saints in the Celtic Church	N. Chadwick	University of Newcastle 1960
Anglo-Saxon Chronicles	Anne Savage ed.	Papermac 1984
Book of Devon	S. Baring-Gould	Methuen 1899
Celt and Saxon	P. Beresford Ellis	Constable 1993
Celtic Alternative	S. Toulson	Rider 1987
Celtic Britain	Charles Thomas	Thames and Hudson 1986
Celtic Christianity	C. Greene	The Internet
Celtic Church	J. Carey	The Internet
Celtic Fire	R. Van de Weyer	Darton, Longman and Todd 1990
Celtic Verse	E. Gill and D. Everett	Blanford 1998
Celtic Way	I. Bradley	Darton, Longman and Todd 1993
Dartmoor Stone Crosses	B. Harrison	Devon Books 2001
Domesday Book – Devon	J. Morris ed.	Phillimore 1985
Early Church in the Landscape	S. Pearce	Archaeological Journal vol. 142, 1985
English Church Dedications	N. Orme	University of Exeter Press 1996
Essays in Cornish History	C. Hendeson	Oxford University Press 1935
Historical Atlas of the South West	Kain and Ravenhill eds.	University of Exeter Press 1999
Holy and Notable Wells of Devon	T. Brown	Transactions of Devonshire Association 1957–1966
Holy Wells of Cornwall	J. Meyrick	Meyrick 1982
Holy Wells of Wales	F. Jones	University of Wales 1992
Letters of Pelagius	Ed. R. Van de Weyer	James 1995
Lives of the British Saints	S. Baring-Gould and J. Fisher	facsimile print by Llanerch 2000
Lives of the Saints Cornwall and Devon	N. Roscarrock ed. N. Orme	Devon and Cornwall Record Society 1992
Place Names in the Landscape	M. Gelling	Dent 1984
Pre-Conquest Church in Devon	C. Raleigh-Radford	Devon Historian vol. 11, 1975
Shrines and Sacrifice	Ann Woodward	English Heritage 1992
St Nectan	G.H. Doble	Devonshire Press 1940
Tavistock Abbey	H.P.R. Finsberg	Cambridge University Press 1951
The Anglo-Saxons	J. Campbell ed.	Penguin Books 1991
The Celtic Saints	N. Pennick	Thorsons 1997
The Heartbeat of God	P. Newell	SPCK 1997
The Living Stream	J. Rattue	Boydell Press 1995
Thousand Years of the English Parish	A. Jones	Windrush Press 2000
Unity and Variety: History of the Church in Devon	N. Orme	University of Exeter Press 1991
Way of the Eagle	J.S. Eriugena (ed. C. Bamford)	Lindisfarne Books 2000